Contemporary Irish Writers

Contemporary Irish Writers and Filmmakers

General Series Editor:
Eugene O'Brien, Head of English Department,
Mary Immaculate College, University of Limerick.

Titles in the series:

Seamus Heaney: Creating Irelands of the Mind
by Eugene O'Brien (Mary Immaculate College, Limerick)

Brian Friel: Decoding the Language of the Tribe
by Tony Corbett

Jim Sheridan: Framing the Nation by Ruth Barton
(University College Dublin)

John Banville: Exploring Fictions by Derek Hand
(St Patrick's College, Drumcondra, Dublin)

Neil Jordan: Exploring Boundaries by Emer Rockett and
Kevin Rockett (Trinity College, Dublin)

Roddy Doyle: Raining on the Parade by Dermot McCarthy
(Huron University College, University of Western Ontario)

Conor McPherson: Imagining Mischief by Gerald Wood
(Carson-Newman College, Tennessee)

William Trevor: Re-imagining Ireland by Mary Fitzgerald-Hoyt
(Siena College, New York)

John McGahern: From the Local to the Universal by
Eamon Maher (Institute of Technology, Tallaght)

Brendan Kennelly: A Host of Ghosts by John McDonagh (Mary
Immaculate College, Limerick)

Forthcoming:
Jennifer Johnston by Shawn O'Hare

Contemporary Irish Writers

Seamus Heaney

Creating Irelands of the Mind

Revised and Updated Edition

Eugene O'Brien

The Liffey Press

Published by The Liffey Press
Ashbrook House, 10 Main Street,
Raheny, Dublin 5, Ireland
www.theliffeypress.com

© 2002, 2005 Eugene O'Brien

A catalogue record of this book is
available from the British Library.

ISBN 1-904148-02-6

Front cover photograph © *The Irish Times*
Reproduced with kind permission

Printed in Spain by Graficas Cems

Contents

About the Author

Eugene O'Brien is Head of the Department of English Language and Literature at Mary Immaculate College, University of Limerick. He is also currently Assistant Dean Research in the College of Humanities, University of Limerick. He is the editor of *The Irish Book Review* and is the Series Editor for The Liffey Press's Contemporary Irish Writers and Filmmakers series, and of the Edwin Mellen Press's *Studies in Irish Literature* and *Irish Studies* series. He has published over 60 articles, chapters and reviews on Irish writing and literary and critical theory. He is author of the following books: *The Question of Irish Identity in the Writings of William Butler Yeats and James Joyce* (1998); *Examining Irish Nationalism in the Context of Literature, Culture and Religion: A Study of the Epistemological Structure of Nationalism* (2002); *Seamus Heaney: Creating Irelands of the Mind* (2002); *Seamus Heaney and the Place of Writing* (2003); *Seamus Heaney: Searches for Answers* (2003). He is editor of three forthcoming books on postcolonialism, globalisation (with Eamon Maher) and theoretical perspectives on Heaney's writing.

Series Introduction

Given the amount of study that the topic of Irish writing, and increasingly Irish film, has generated, perhaps the first task of a series entitled *Contemporary Irish Writers and Film-makers* is to justify its existence in a time of diminishing rainforests. As Declan Kiberd's *Irish Classics* has shown, Ireland has produced a great variety of writers who have influenced indigenous, and indeed, world culture, and there are innumerable books devoted to the study of the works of Yeats, Joyce and Beckett. These writers spoke out of a particular Irish culture, and also transcended that culture to speak to the Anglophone world, and beyond.

Ireland, however, has undergone a paradigm shift in the last twenty years. Economically, politically and culturally, it is a vastly different place to the Ireland of Yeats and Joyce. In the light of the fundamentally altered nature of the Diasporic experience, definitions of Irishness and of identity are being rewritten in a more positive light. Irish people now emigrate to well-paid jobs, working in high rise offices in London and New York, a far cry from previous generations whose hard physical labour built those self-same offices. At the same time, the new-found wealth at home has been complemented by a growing multiculturalism, challenging perspectives on identity like never before.

Modes and worldviews inherited from the past no longer seem adequate to describe an increasingly cosmopolitan and complex society. This is the void which Contemporary Irish Writers and Filmmakers hopes to fill by providing an examination of the state of contemporary cultural Ireland through an analysis of its writers and filmmakers.

The role of the aesthetic in the shaping of attitudes and opinions cannot be understated and these books will attempt to understand the transformative potential of the work of the artist in the context of the ongoing redefinition of society and culture. The current proliferation of writers and filmmakers of the highest quality can be taken as an index of the growing confidence of this society, and in the desire to enunciate that confidence. However, as Luke Gibbons has put it: "a people has not found its voice until it has expressed itself, not only in a body of creative works, but also in a body of critical works," and Contemporary Irish Writers and Filmmakers is part of such an attempt to find that voice.

Aimed at the student and general reader alike, this series will analyse and examine the major texts, themes and topics that have been addressed by these present-day voices. At another level, each book will trace the effect of a specific artist on the mindset of Irish people.

It is hoped that this series will encourage discussion and debate about issues that have engaged the writers and filmmakers who enunciate, and transform, contemporary Irish culture. It is further hoped that the series will play its part in enabling our continuing participation in the great humanistic project of understanding ourselves and others.

Eugene O'Brien
Department of English
Mary Immaculate College
University of Limerick

Acknowledgements

This book is an updated version of the edition published in 2002. It is necessitated by a number of new works by Seamus Heaney which were not addressed in the original version. I have made very few changes to the chapters on Heaney's other books, not because the opinions are unchanging, but because if I started, this would become a different book. I would like to thank my wife, Áine McElhinney, who remains my most acute proof-reader and critic, as well as being a constant source of support and encouragement, for all her help, and for putting up with me, and very late nights, during this revision. Brian Langan and David Givens of The Liffey Press were supportive of this book, and the series in general, from the outset and I am grateful for this and for their professionalism and efficiency. Many of the ideas in this series about contemporary Irish culture have been rehearsed in formal and informal discussions with members of the Department of English Language and Literature in Mary Immaculate College, and I would like to thank in particular two doctoral students, Eoin Flannery and Paula Murphy, whose work has taught me as much as I have taught them. Eoin, Dara and Sinéad were an ongoing inspiration during the writing of this book, while Paul and Katie were, and are, a constant presence.

To Áine, Dara, Sinéad and Eoin

Chronology

1939	Seamus Justin Heaney born on April 13, the eldest of nine children born to Patrick and Margaret Heaney. The family live on a farm in Mossbawn, County Derry, in Northern Ireland.
1945	Attends Anahorish primary school, with both Protestant and Catholic pupils.
1947	Northern Ireland Education Act makes access to second level education more universally available, especially for Catholics.
1949	Republic of Ireland is established, and immediately leaves the British Commonwealth. The Ireland Act guarantees Northern Ireland's position within the United Kingdom.
1951	Heaney wins a scholarship to Saint Columb's College in Derry.
1951–57	Attends Saint Columb's College as a boarder, where he meets Seamus Deane, writer and critic. Other graduates of the college include the SDLP politician John Hume and the playwright Brian Friel.
1953	Heaney's four-year-old brother, Christopher, is killed in a car accident.

1954	Flags and Emblems Act introduced in Northern Ireland, prohibiting the flying of the "tricolour" (the flag of the Republic of Ireland).
1956–62	The Irish Republican Army (IRA) begins its "border campaign". As a result, internment is introduced in both Northern Ireland and the Republic of Ireland.
1957–61	Heaney attends Queen's University Belfast on a "State Exhibition" bursary. He obtains a First Class Honours in English Language and Literature, winning the McMullen Medal.
1959	First poems published in Queen's literary magazines *Q* and *Gorgon*, as is a short story, *There's Rosemary*.
1961–62	Attends Saint Joseph's College of Education in Andersonstown, having decided against postgraduate work at Oxford. Writes an extended essay on Ulster literary magazines, "In Our Own Dour Way".
1962	Teaches at Saint Thomas's Intermediate School in Ballymurphy, Belfast.
1962–63	Undertakes part-time postgraduate work at Queen's and begins lecturing at Saint Joseph's College of Education.
1963	Becomes a member of the Belfast Group, set up by Philip Hobsbaum, where poets read and critique each other's work.
1964	Campaign for Social Justice formed to highlight incidences of discrimination against Catholics.
1965	Marries Marie Devlin of Ardboe, County Tyrone. First official meeting between the Northern Ireland Prime Minister Terence O'Neill and the Republic of Ireland Taoiseach Sean Lemass.

1966	His son Michael is born; *Death of a Naturalist* published; becomes a lecturer at Queen's University. Rioting in Belfast as a protest against 1916 commemoration. Ulster Volunteer Force shoot a Catholic and plant a bomb in County Down. The IRA blows up Nelson's Pillar in Dublin.
1967	Heaney receives the Eric Gregory Award and the Cholmondeley Award. The Northern Ireland Civil Rights Association is formed to demand "one man one vote" and to remove other anomalies that discriminate against Catholics.
1968	His son Christopher is born. Civil rights marches stopped by police. Receives the Somerset Maugham Award, and the Geoffrey Faber Memorial Prize.
1969	*Door into the Dark* published. British troops sent into Belfast and Derry. Heaney is in Europe as part of Somerset Maugham Award.
1970–71	Spends a year as guest lecturer in the University of California at Berkeley.
1971	Internment is introduced in Northern Ireland with some 1,500 people being interned.
1972	30 January, Bloody Sunday: British Paratroopers kill thirteen unarmed civil rights marchers and wound twelve more. Serious rioting in nationalist areas of Northern Ireland. In August, the Heaneys move to a cottage in Glanmore, County Wicklow in the Republic of Ireland. *Wintering Out* is published. Receives the Irish-American Cultural Foundation Award.
1973	His daughter, Catherine Ann, is born. Receives the Denis Devlin Award.
1975	*North* is published. He joins the faculty of Carysfort Training College. Receives E.M. Forster Award.

1976	Family move to Sandymount in Dublin. Awarded Duff Cooper Memorial Prize.
1979	*Field Work* published. He spends a term at Harvard.
1980	*Preoccupations* and *Selected Poems* are published.
1980–81	Ten republican prisoners die on hunger strike protesting about their lack of political status in prison.
1981	Joins Field Day, with Stephen Rea and Brian Friel, in Derry.
1982	Begins five-year contract at Harvard and publishes *The Rattle Bag*, with Ted Hughes. Receives Bennett Award. Receives honorary D.Litt. from Queen's University.
1983	*Sweeney Astray*, a translation of the medieval Irish language poem *Buile Shuibhne*, is published by Field Day, as is *An Open Letter*, a verse pamphlet in which Heaney objects to being called a British poet in Morrison and Motion's *Penguin Anthology of Contemporary British Poetry*. *Among Schoolchildren* lecture is published. Receives Lannan Foundation Award.
1984	*Station Island* published, and Heaney becomes Boylston Professor of Rhetoric and Oratory in Harvard. His mother, Margaret, dies in October.
1986	His father, Patrick, dies in October.
1987	*The Haw Lantern* published.
1988	*The Government of the Tongue* published. Heaney is elected as Professor of Poetry at Oxford.
1989	*The Place of Writing* published.
1990	*The Cure at Troy* (translation of Sophocles' *Philoctetes*) published. The play is performed by Field Day in Derry. New volume of *Selected Poems 1966–1987* published.

1991	*Seeing Things* published.
1994	Provisional IRA ceasefire begins in Northern Ireland.
1995	Heaney is awarded the Nobel Prize for literature. *Crediting Poetry*, the Nobel lecture, is published. *The Redress of Poetry* (selection of his Oxford lectures) published. A joint translation, with Stanisław Barańczak, of Jan Kochanowski's *Laments* published.
1996	*The Spirit Level* published. IRA end ceasefire.
1997	*The Spirit Level* wins the Whitbread Prize. IRA ceasefire re-established.
1998	*Opened Ground: Poems 1966–1996* published. April 10: Good Friday Agreement signed. August 15: Omagh bomb explodes, killing 29 people and injuring 220.
1999	*Beowulf*, translation of the Anglo-Saxon epic, is published.
2000	*Beowulf* wins Whitbread Poetry Award. Publication of *The Midnight Verdict*, a translation of a selection from Brian Merriman's *Cúirt an Mheán Oíche* and Ovid's *Metamorphoses*.
2001	*Electric Light* published.
2002	*Finders Keepers: Selected Prose* published.
2004	*The Burial at Thebes: Sophocles' Antigone* published.
2004	*Room to Rhyme* published.
2004	*Anything Can Happen* published.
2005	*The Door Stands Open* published.

List of Abbreviations

AH: Anything Can Happen
AS: Among Schoolchildren
B: Beowulf
BT: The Burial at Thebes
CP: Crediting Poetry
CT: The Cure at Troy
DID: Door into the Dark
DON: Death of a Naturalist
EI: Envies and Identifications: Dante and the Modern Poet
EL: Electric Light
ER: Earning a Rhyme
FK: Finders Keepers
FW: Field Work
GT: The Government of the Tongue
HL: The Haw Lantern
L: Laments
LE: Learning from Eliot
MV: The Midnight Verdict
N: North
OL: An Open Letter
P: Preoccupations
PD: Place and Displacement
PW: The Place of Writing
RP: The Redress of Poetry
SA: Sweeney Astray
SI: Station Island
SL: The Spirit Level
WO: Wintering Out

Introduction

Perhaps the first requirement of any new book on the work of Seamus Heaney is that it should justify its existence. There are over thirty full-length studies of Heaney already published. The number of articles in journals and conference papers on his work exceeds those on any other contemporary writer. There are overviews, thematically driven studies, articles that focus on particular groups of poems and discussions of his biography. So, yet another book on Heaney, part of what Desmond Fennell has called the "Heaney phenomenon", raises the obvious question: what it can bring to our appreciation of this poet?

Despite Heaney's widespread popularity and phenomenal sales (print-runs of seven or eight times those of other poetry books), there remains a consensual reading of him as a poet of "muddy-booted blackberry picking" (Ricks, 1969: 900–1) whose most famous work is *North*, wherein he voices the "tragedy of a people in a place", namely "the Catholics of Northern Ireland" (Cruise O'Brien, 1976: 404). Much of the critical work on Heaney still focuses on the early poems, and on the political perspective of his writing. However, it is well to remember that the early books were written in 1966 (*Death of a Naturalist*) and 1969 (*Door into the Dark*), with *North* being published as long ago as 1975.

The importance of these books cannot be denied, and in the present study, I will be examining how Heaney progressed from a personal vision of digging into his familial past to a more Jungian view of digging into the historical consciousness of his psyche. However, I will also be suggesting that to see *North* in particular, and Heaney's books in general, as in any way representing a simplistic nationalistic outlook is to misread them completely. I will argue that these books adopt a far more complex attitude to issues of nationalism, Catholicism and Irishness.

This probing and questioning of the past, and of received ideas, is perhaps the most important intellectual activity that is taking place in contemporary Ireland. Since the achievement of independence from Britain in 1922, and the establishment of the Republic of Ireland in 1949, Ireland has trodden the traditional postcolonial path of replacing the hierarchy of the coloniser with a native elite who were similarly seen to be above and beyond question. As a result, in the years since independence, the power structures of church and state remained almost totally immune from criticism or from interrogation, and it is only in recent years that an increasingly educated population has come to call into question the decisions, actions and, on occasion, criminal acts of the leaders of church and state.

This process, which, I would suggest, is necessary for the growth of a healthy democracy, has left many of the old certainties in tatters, and many people in a similar state of doubt as regards principles, values and ethical positions. Heaney's probings of the seeming certainties of the past, his ongoing questioning of the nature of his Irishness, of his Catholic inheritance and of his sense of nationalism has been salutary in terms of the psychic growth of Ireland. Heaney's work encapsulates many of the dilemmas experienced by contemporary Irish people. Many can identify with the postmodern *angst* of being "lost, / Unhappy and at home" (*WO,*

48), or with the sense of uncertainty captured by his response to the Northern Irish "troubles": "I am neither internee nor informer" (*N*, 73). In terms of the sense of doubt created by the ongoing questioning of received values, again Heaney captures the prevailing mood: "We're on shifting sand. It is all sea-change. / Clear one minute. Next minute haze" (*CT*, 12). As many Irish people began to question the nature of their inheritance of nationalism and republicanism during the ongoing violence of the 1970s and 1980s, Heaney again voiced an almost universal feeling of hopelessness: "Our island is full of comfortless noises" (*FW*, 13).

It was no accident that, during the peace process negotiations, Heaney's words from *The Cure at Troy* became almost a catch-phrase: "And hope and history rhyme" (*CT*, 77). Heaney is all too aware of the fragile nature of ceasefires, where "exhaustions nominated peace" (*N*, 20), and he is unwilling to completely endorse a view that would see all of the violence of the past thirty years as finished. In "Mycenae Lookout", he aptly describes the attitude of a soldier of Troy, still doing his sentry duty, still caught in the rhythms of war: "I felt the beating of the huge time-wound / We lived inside" (*SL*, 34). It is a tribute to the skill of his writing, and a sign of the importance of his work, that he is able to understand the depth of this wound, while at the same time stressing the necessity of achieving a position outside this historically driven structure.

It is this ability to encompass in a felicitous phrase the problems that are of central importance to Irish people that is so important in Heaney's work. Just as we as a nation have been slow to develop any sense of self-confidence, so Heaney too has waited until he was "nearly fifty / To credit marvels" (*ST*, 50). It is also significant that, even in this new ability to credit marvels, Heaney is still asking awkward questions, and setting out the need for "different states of mind // At different times" (*ST*, 97) to cope with the complexity of contemporary life. In terms of the journey he has undertaken, from his own early home in the "three rooms of a traditional thatched farmstead" (*CP*, 9) to his place at the podium in Stockholm as he accepted the Nobel Prize for Literature, he has paralleled the psychic journey that has been undertaken by contemporary Ireland, as we become central figures in a developing European Union, while retaining our Anglophone connections with America, and becoming less restricted by the heritage of our past, as we look towards the future. As Heaney puts it, despite the "dolorous circumstances" of his native place, he "straightened up" and felt the urge to express his desire that the physical borders that divided Ireland may take on the nature of the "net on a tennis court", allowing for a deal of "agile give-and-take, for encounter and contending", which might, in time, allow for a "less binary and altogether less binding vocabulary" (*CP*, 23).

So, to return to the question with which I began: this book justifies itself by suggesting reasons for the importance of the work of Seamus Heaney in terms of the Ireland of today. I would suggest that Heaney's development, as I will chart it in this study, parallels and anticipates that of the Irish psyche over the past fifty years. Heaney has progressed in terms of his thinking from a relatively simplistic and conventional perspective into a far more cosmopolitan and complex view of his own identity. His developing writing, encompassing, as it does, influences from different cultures, languages and texts, enacts a movement from "prying into roots" and "fingering slime" to an embrace of different aspects of European and world culture which has strong parallels with the development of Ireland itself.

From being a backward, inward-looking country, obsessed with the past and with a sense of inferiority, Ireland has begun, in the words of Robert Emmet, to take her place among the nations of the earth. By this, I do not just mean in economic terms, as evidenced by the much-lauded Celtic

Tiger phenomenon. I also mean in cultural, social and intellectual terms, as we become more confident of our place in
Europe, and of our position as a bridge between Europe and
America. Because the thrust of my argument suggests a parallel between the development of Heaney's own thought and
the developing sense of self-consciousness and sophistication
of contemporary Ireland, my approach will be broadly
chronological, grouping different works into different stages
of development. While such a procedure is necessarily arbi-
trary, nevertheless I feel that there is an internal coherence
in the groups of texts which I have chosen.

Hence, the opening chapter will study his early work:
Death of a Naturalist, Door into the Dark, Wintering Out and
North. In this chapter, we will examine how the probing of
his personal past gradually developed into a probing of the
psychic past of Ireland, with particular emphasis on the na-
tionalist-republican narrative of history. Heaney's "bog poems", which span the first four books, albeit in different
forms, have formed a powerful symbol of the racial memory
of the nationalist community, a memory which allowed violence to thrive in the thirty years of the Northern Irish
"troubles".

Chapter Two will examine *Field Work, An Open Letter,
Sweeney Astray* and *Station Island* in terms of their development of issues introduced in the earlier books. In these
books, there is a change of focus as the mythological *persona*
of the first four books leads to a more personal voice, with
the "I" in these poems referring more concretely to the
contemporary Heaney, now living in Glanmore in County
Wicklow, and later in Dublin.

The third chapter will examine *The Haw Lantern* and *Seeing Things*, demonstrating how different preoccupations have
been thematically and formally developed in these collections. They are central to his process of self-interrogation,
acting as a hinge, what Derrida terms a *brisure*, which open

out his new sense of the complexity of the self by questioning the validity of origins. Here, he develops the idea that
"the idea of a centre is fictive" (Deane, 1996: 28). The level
of development in terms of a more cosmopolitan style, a
greater fluency of reference, and a clearer vision of the possibilities inherent in present and future will be further explored.

Chapter Four will focus on Heaney's translations in
terms of text and of theory. *The Spirit Level* is full of translations in the sense of crossings, delicately achieved balances
and an increasing focus on the process of movement between different points. In *The Cure at Troy*, he takes this process a stage further, using the characters of Philoctetes and
Neoptolemus as analogues of the situation in Northern
Ireland. He proceeds this exploration apace with his very
specific translation of Sophocles' *Antigone* in *The Burial at
Thebes*, which is also discussed in terms of the conflict between the individual and the group. His translation of Jan
Kochanowski's *Laments* and his version of Brian Merriman's
The Midnight Court, itself framed by two translations from
Ovid, combine to offer a theory of the value of translation in
an increasingly multi-cultural society. Using the language of
the other allows for an ethical turn in his work, paralleling
the ideas of Emmanuel Levinas.

Chapter Five will examine his major collections of prose:
Preoccupations, *The Government of the Tongue*, *The Redress of
Poetry*, *Finders Keepers*, and the introduction to his translation
of *Beowulf* in order to explore the thinking behind the poetry. His increasing openness to other cultures is clear, as is
his desire to create verbal structures which are adequate to
the complex structures of identity which he is enunciating. It
will also examine his recent essay and translation, *Anything
Can Happen*, written as a partial response to the events of
September 11th 2001.

Finally, Chapter Six will examine his latest collection, *Electric Light*, in terms of its overall importance in Heaney's writing. The Ireland of the twenty-first century is vastly different to the Ireland in which Heaney began to write in the 1960s. He has made the point that "an inheritance" is from "the long ago" (*ST*, 28), and yet it can be made "willable forward / Again and again and again", because "whatever is given // Can always be reimagined" (*ST*, 29). I would suggest that one of his own most important contributions to the intellectual development that has taken place in this country is that ability to take the inheritance of the past — colonialism, nationalism, the Catholic Church, the Diaspora, language — and to reimagine the effect and influence of these aspects of tradition for the present and the future.

So (to use a Heaneyism), to answer the initial question with which we began, this book justifies its existence by examining the development of Heaney's writing — in poetry, prose and translation — and by demonstrating the relationship between this aesthetic development and the development of consciousness in contemporary Ireland. As he puts it in "On Poetry and Professing", "if it is a delusion and a danger to expect poetry and music to do too much, it is a diminishment of them and a derogation to ignore what they can do" (*FK*, 69).

Chapter One

Northern Exposure:
Digging into the Past

Among the most famous opening lines of any modern poem are those of "Digging": "Between my finger and my thumb / The squat pen rests; snug as a gun" (*DON*, 13). These lines have been taken as an artistic *credo* in which Heaney stresses a type of writing through which he will undertake an exploration of his personal past. The "digging" in question here is an activity for which the Heaneys as a family were well known, and Heaney has flagged its importance, despite calling it a "big coarse-grained navvy of a poem" (*P*, 43), by seeing it as the first instance where his "feel had got into words" (*P*, 41). The critics have generally agreed.

Elmer Andrews sees the poem as ending in affirmation (Andrews, 1988: 40), while Robert Buttel sees the end of the poem as equating pen and spade under the rubric of both implements' "precise, efficient mastery" (Buttel, 1975: 37). For Blake Morrison, Heaney's own implement performs many of the same functions as that of his father: "passing on tradition, extracting 'new' produce (poems, not potatoes) out of old furrows, and enjoying an intimacy with the earth" (Morrison, 1982: 27), while Michael Parker attempts to assign a reconciling function to the "living roots" image by noting that it symbolises the reconciliation between "the traditional labour of his forefathers with his newly discovered vocation" (Parker, 1993: 63).

In this poem, three male generations of Heaneys are mentioned. The poet's father, digging in the flowerbeds is being watched by Heaney, who, with a pen between his finger and thumb, is writing and looking out through his window. In the second stanza, this naturalistic view of his father is imaginatively transposed back in time in the memory of the watching Heaney: "Till his straining rump among the flowerbeds / Bends low, comes up twenty years away", digging potatoes. This movement, achieved by the use of a time measurement, "years", as opposed to the expected spatial measurement (yards), allows Heaney to think back to a past time, when his father was younger and when Heaney himself was only a child. This temporal reversion in turn is the hinge that allows the third member of the family to appear, again connected by the image of digging:

> By God, the old man could handle a spade.
> Just like his old man.
>
> My grandfather cut more turf in a day
> Than any other man on Toner's bog. (*DON*, 13)

The fact that the initial two lines are end-stopped, and that the second "sentence" is grammatically not a sentence, draws our attention to the connection that is being created between son, father and grandfather. This connection is reinforced and developed by the items which they are digging: "flowers . . . potatoes . . . turf" and the places wherein they are working: "flowerbeds . . . potato drills . . . bog". This movement, from flowers (beauty) to potatoes (food) to turf (beginnings) could be seen to anticipate the later mythic bog poems, a fact which underlines the importance of this poem in Heaney's canon. Having made the connection between son and father, Heaney goes on to recall a connection with his grandfather in a remembered incident even further back in time, as he recalls that "once" he had carried "milk in a bottle" to his grandfather, and remembers his grandfather drinking deeply and then returning to the activity which connects all three: "Digging" (*DON,* 14). Again, this one-word "sentence", while defying grammatical convention, stresses the importance of this verb as both a description of a physical activity as well as a symbol of connectedness between Heaney and his forbears.

Having connected all three generations, the poem, in the penultimate and final stanzas, gives an almost cinematic series of images recalling the different types of digging, before achieving a climactic conclusion which repeats aspects of the opening lines, but with an important difference:

> The cold smell of potato mould, the squelch and slap
> Of soggy peat, the curt cuts of an edge
> Through living roots awaken in my head.
> But I've no spade to follow men like them.
>
> Between my finger and my thumb
> The squat pen rests.
> I'll dig with it. (*DON,* 14)

The order of these images is inverted in terms of the original occurrence in the poem. We remember that in the earlier stanzas, the first digging was in a flowerbed, the second in the potato drills, while the third was in "Toner's bog". In the stanza quoted above, we move from potato drills to the bog and back to the flowerbeds, which are under the writing poet's window, and thence to the poet. The movement is almost like a camera panning from image to image before finally focusing in close-up on the poet, and then entering into his mind, with the line stressing that, as he has no spade to carry on the tradition, he will instead use a pen to dig, a metaphor which will gradually unfold throughout his work. At another level, repeating the opening couplet and stressing the word "dig" brings the closing line into direct contrast with the "snug as a gun" line: not only is he choosing the pen over the spade; he is also choosing the pen as a means of digging, rather than using it as a metaphorical gun.

Critical commentary on the poem has recognised its importance. Andrew Waterman sees the poem as a personal artistic manifesto, which claims continuities and analogues between Heaney's own writing, and the "manual skills and livelihoods of his forebears" (Waterman, 1992: 12). Neil Corcoran, having noted the centrality of the pen/spade metaphor, speaks of a "willed continuity between spade and pen" (Corcoran, 1998: 51); while Elmer Andrews observes the poet celebrating the diggers' "intimacy with the land", and sees Heaney as attempting to replicate this artesian experience in his writing as he "delves into his experience to produce poems" (Andrews, 1988: 38–39).

The familial connection is important, as he goes on to see this poem as letting down "a shaft into real life" (*P*, 41). This artesian perspective is one which will inform his first four books of poetry: *Death of a Naturalist* (1966); *Door into the Dark* (1969); *Wintering Out* (1972); and *North* (1975). He has spoken at length in different interviews about the sense of connection between these books, telling John Haffenden that:

> I'm certain that up to *North*, that that was one book; in a way it grows together and goes together. There has been a good bit of commentary about the metaphor of digging and going back, but luckily that was unselfconscious . . . the kind of unselfconsciousness that poets approaching the age of forty know they won't have again! (Haffenden, 1981: 64)

All of the bog poems, which span the early books, and the archaeological poems, which are to be found in the opening sections of *Wintering Out* and *North*, can be seen as the fruits of this downward and backward poetic vector. They result from Heaney's attempt to "go on from a personal, rural childhood poetry" and make "wider connections, public connections" (Randall, 1979: 16), a project that would be both structural and thematic.

"At a Potato Digging" is an example of this process of widening the focus of the poetry. The opening two sections of this poem seem to carry on the naturalistic descriptions that we saw in "Digging", as the rhymed quatrains describe the physicality of the act of digging potatoes. Here, however, there is a change of pace, as the digging is no longer done with a spade but by a "mechanical digger" which "wrecks the drill" (*DON*, 31) as it unearths the new potatoes. But there are also new mythic tones here that would seem to place this poem as a precursor to the darker bog poems of *North* and *Wintering Out*.

In this poem, a strong mythic and religious note is created through the gradual build-up of imagery:

> Heads bow, trunks bend, hands fumble towards the black
> Mother. (*DON*, 31)

Here, the initial matter of "Digging" — soil and turf — is given a historical and mythic resonance, and we get our first glimpse of the earth as a mother goddess, a trope which, as I have suggested, will echo throughout his bog poems. There is also an implied critique of religion in the image of the "muscles" in the backs of the "humbled knees" being strengthened. It is as if a religious mindset, which accepts the voice of authority, is no longer seen as a necessarily good thing. In a manner redolent of the poetic technique of "Digging", the temporal shift that occurs between sections II and

III of the poem makes explicit the implied associations between the contemporary present of the poem, and the potato famine of the 1800s in Ireland, when hundreds of thou-
sands died. He also makes use of personification, a rhetorical
figure which attributes the qualities of life to inanimate objects. In the hinge between sections II and III, Heaney also
makes use of chiasmus, a crossing over and repetition of the
same terms for the purpose of changing their effect. He is
talking about "knots of potatoes" which taste of "ground
and root" and goes on to describe how they will be stored:

> To be piled in pits; live skulls, blind-eyed

> III
> Live skulls, blind-eyed, balanced on
> wild higgledy skeletons
> scoured the land in 'forty-five. (*DON*, 32)

This cinematic cutting from present to past and from description to imaginative reconstruction has been carefully pre-
pared for by an image chain of "a dark shower . . . Fingers go
dead in the cold . . . A higgledy line" (*DON*, 31) as well as by
the overt religious imagery already cited. This poem, while
strong on description and innovative in technique, has an unresolved quality, as if the image of the famine victims is an
imaginative flashback, caused by associations of land and history: "where potato diggers are / you still smell the running
sore" (*DON*, 33). Here, the power of the past to remain ac-
tive in the present, a trope first seen in "Digging", is the major point of the poem, and it is a point which underscores
the duality of perspective in Heaney's artesian imagination.

Henry Hart, writing about this poem, sees it as an elegy
for the famine victims "that places the human deaths into
the larger context of nature's ineluctable, regenerative
rhythm" (Hart, 1992: 28). This description could apply just
as well to any of Heaney's bog poems. Indeed, I would argue

that this could well be seen as the initial bog poem, containing many of the elements of these poems, which are generally seen to stretch across *Door into the Dark*, *Wintering Out* and *North*. The initial bog poem, "Bogland" appears as the closing poem of *Door into the Dark*; with "Nerthus" and "The Tollund Man" appearing in *Wintering Out*; and a six-poem sequence appearing in Part 1 of *North*. In all of these, there is a double perspective, a binocularity of vision — of the land as a physical entity, which hoards items and objects from the past within itself; and of the land as symbolic of the psychic racial memory of the nationalist consciousness, with the objects that have been excavated becoming symbolic of images of pain and victimhood which have been hoarded within the psychic memory.

"Bogland", like the other poems we have been discussing, has its origins in the digging metaphor. In "Digging" the poetic voice was singular; it was the voice of a mature Heaney recalling memories of events that had occurred when he was younger. The focus of the poem was on the relationship between the "I" and his family and his tradition. In "Bogland", the pronoun has become transformed, and the poem begins: "We have no prairies / To slice a big sun at evening — " (*DID*, 55), as Heaney locates himself firmly as part of a group which defines itself negatively against the vast open spaces of the American prairies. There, the pioneers moved forward and outward across the continent, defining themselves and their country in the process. In Ireland, he seems to be saying, such a progress is not possible:

> Our pioneers keep striking
> Inwards and downwards,
>
> Every layer they strip
> Seems camped on before.
> The bogholes might be Atlantic seepage.
> The wet centre is bottomless. (*DID*, 56)

"Inwards and downwards" encapsulates the direction of the imagination in the first four books. In an interview with Caroline Walsh, Heaney makes the connection explicit, noting that in this poem there is "an attempt to link, in a symbolic Jungian way" the bog as the "repository and memory of the landscape, with the psyche of the people" (Walsh, 1976: 5). Just as the soil of his own home in "Digging" seemed to hold the memories of his father and grandfather, so, in a broader sense, the bog is seen as an image of the social unconscious of Ireland. This connection between a people and their land would be further probed in his "Requiem for the Croppies", a poem which made play of a reported fact that when the rebels who died on Vinegar Hill in County Wexford in 1798 were buried in common graves, "these graves began to sprout with young barley, growing up from barley corn which the 'croppies' had carried in their pockets to eat while on the march" (*P*, 56). That such seeds could be metaphorical as well as literal is an image which will be more fully developed in his "bog poems". In this sense, Heaney is voicing that widespread acceptance of a teleology of nationalist history which saw the seeds of republicanism handed down through the generations until the national will achieved independence.

Heaney made the point, in 1979, that his leaving of Northern Ireland in 1972, some three years after *Door into the Dark* was published, was viewed in some quarters with a "sense of almost betrayal", adding that the political situation had generated "a great energy and group loyalty" as well as a "defensiveness about its own verities" (Randall, 1979: 8). Significantly, in terms of these discussions of group loyalty, and of the transformation of perspective from the singular to the communal plural, Heaney stresses the importance of "Bogland" in a manner which recalls his "shaft into real life" comment concerning "Digging":

the bog was a genuine obsession. It was an illiterate pleasure that I took in the landscape. The smell of turf smoke, for example, has a terrific nostalgic effect on me. It has to do with the script that's written into your senses from the minute you begin to breathe. Now for me, "bogland" is an important word in that script and the first poem I ever wrote that seemed to me to have elements of the symbolic about it was "Bogland". (Randall, 1979: 17–18)

The importance of "Bogland", then, is that it is a further page in the script that was imprinted in Heaney in terms of the widening circles of family, community and culture. It is as if he is beginning to write from within his culture, and to fuse "the psychic self-searching of poet and nation" (Longley, 1986: 144). As he puts it in *Preoccupations*, he had a need to "make a congruence between memory and bogland" and "our national consciousness" (*P*, 54–5).

The symbolism of the bog as a hoarder of these objects is expanded by Heaney into the realm of images and ideas. As he puts it, he imagines "the imagination itself sinking endlessly down and under that heathery expanse" (Broadbridge, 1977: 39). The bottomlessness of the "wet centre" implies that this process of exploration will never find an origin, that any attempt at an authoritative account of the bog will be doomed to failure. Here, the image of discontinuity that we saw in the "curt cuts of an edge" image in "Digging" is further indicated, as what Andrew Murphy has called the "heterogeneity of the bog" (Murphy, 2000a: 36) is highlighted. It preserves whatever happens to fall into it, allowing multiple historical narratives to emerge. The idea of the bog as an ideologically directed memory bank has not yet come into being for Heaney, although this would gradually come into being through his reading of P.V. Glob's *The Bog People*, and through his feelings of obligation that he should confront the ongoing violence in Northern Ireland.

Heaney published *Door into the Dark* in 1969, and it was
in this year that the "troubles" in Northern Ireland began in
earnest. There was a certain amount of pressure on poets
and writers to "respond" to these, especially given the sustained media interest in the conflict. The roots of this situation can be traced to the 1947 Education Act, which had
opened third-level education to a generation of nationalists.
Generally speaking, Northern Ireland, as a state, was domi-
nated by a Protestant majority whose major fear was being
co-opted into a 32-county Ireland. It was created through a
partitioning of Ireland in the Treaty of 1922. Seeing themselves as constantly under threat by the Catholic and nationalist 26-county state, a situation made more overt by the
withdrawal of the Republic of Ireland from the Commonwealth, the unionist and loyalist majority ensured domina-
tion of all areas of the Stormont government, with, for example, Protestants holding 95 per cent of top public service
positions.

With an increasing number of nationalists being educated to degree level, and keeping in mind the libertarian
climate of the 1960s and the access brought by the media to
the Civil Rights movement in the United States, it is hardly
surprising that the Northern Ireland Civil Rights Association
was formed in 1967. The demands were in keeping with a
liberal agenda: reform of voting rights in local elections (only
rate payers had the vote until then); an end to gerrymander-
ing of constituency boundaries (the action of manipulating
the boundaries of a constituency in order to give an unfair
advantage at an election to a particular party or class); reform of housing allocations and public sector appointments;
the repeal of the Special Powers Act and the disbandment of
the all-Protestant, paramilitary-style B-Special police force.
Because the Civil Rights Association did not inform the police of the planned marches, their marches were declared

illegal. In 1968, the first civil rights march, from Coalisland to Dungannon, was held in August, and passed peacefully.

However, another march, on 5 October, was stopped by the Royal Ulster Constabulary, who baton-charged the crowd, injuring some of the marchers. Two days of rioting followed, and this incident is seen by many as the beginning of the present "troubles". Both the march and the rioting were filmed, and this drew the attention of the world's media to Belfast, and embarrassed both the unionist power structure and the British government. The presence of the media, a point highlighted in Heaney's discursive "Whatever You Say Say Nothing", in *North*, was of central importance in bringing this conflict to the attention of the world. On 1 January 1969, a four-day march from Belfast to Derry was begun, an idea paralleling Martin Luther King's march from Selma to Montgomery, Alabama. On the fourth day, the march was attacked by loyalists, including some off-duty B-Specials, at Burntollet Bridge.

The resultant publicity fractured the previously mono-lithic Unionist Party, with some unionists looking to appease nationalist demands and recapture world opinion, while others were reluctant to make any changes in the *status quo*. In the election of 1969, 27 Official Unionists and 12 Unofficial Unionists were elected. A further flashpoint was the Apprentice Boys parade (commemorating the barring of the gates of the city against James II in 1688) which took place in Derry. As the parade passed close to the Nationalist Bogside area, serious rioting erupted:

> The Royal Ulster Constabulary (RUC), using ar-
> moured cars and water cannons, entered the
> Bogside, to end the rioting. What was to become
> known as the Battle of the Bogside lasted for two
> days, and rioting spread throughout the north. In
> Belfast, streets of houses were burned down by

> rioters and over 3,500 families, mainly Catholics,
> were driven from their homes. Seven people were
> killed and one hundred wounded as the rioters be-
> gan to use guns. The riots spread across Northern
> Ireland . . . on August 15, the UK prime minister
> Harold Wilson ordered the British Army into Belfast
> and Derry to support the RUC. Four days later he
> also ordered the Stormont government to introduce
> "one man one vote", disband the B-specials, and dis-
> arm and restructure the RUC. (O'Brien, 2001: 229)

During these riots, the IRA demand for a united Ireland was rekindled, and a demand arose from within Catholic and nationalist communities for a defence of their areas against attack. Up until then, the IRA had been largely moribund, with many of the activists drifting towards left-wing socialist policies and away from violence. During the Sinn Féin *Ard Fheis* (party conference) of December 1969, the organisation split into the Official IRA and the Provisional IRA. The more militant PIRA began an aggressive campaign for money and arms, receiving both from sympathisers in the Republic and in the United States. The PIRA proclaimed the RUC and B-Specials to be "legitimate targets" and became increasingly involved in civilian demonstrations and riots:

> Twenty-five people were killed in 1970 and 174 in
> 1971. By mid-1970, the PIRA were believed to be
> around 1,500 strong, and there were 153 explosions
> in 1970, escalating to 304 explosions in the first six
> months of 1971. The violence in Northern Ireland
> worsened in 1972, with 467 people killed. (O'Brien,
> 2001: 230)

Perhaps the most frightening aspect of this situation was the alacrity with which seemingly dormant sectarian hatreds came to the surface, and the speed with which communities became polarised. It was as if hatred and a sense of victimhood or persecution had remained lodged in the memories of the two communities, waiting, like a Freudian return of the repressed, to unleash themselves again.

Given Heaney's increasing sense of identification with his own community — the movement from "I" to "we" — in "Bogland", the notion of racial or psychic memory that he touched on in this poem was further reinforced when he read Glob's *The Bog People*, a book which "provided a foundation for many diverse later developments" (Wade, 1993: 37). As Michael Parker tells us, as soon as Heaney saw photographs from the book, he immediately sent for it as it embraced a number of his deepest concerns: "landscape, religion, sexuality, violence, history, myth" (Parker, 1993: 91). That this symbol was so intimately connected with his own personal bogland myth meant that it would become a further development of the digging motif which we have been exploring.

As Heaney has noted, there was a sense in which the writers in Northern Ireland were expected to respond to the conflict in their work: "a simple minded pressure also to speak up for their own side" (Donnelly, 1977: 60), and clearly this pressure was felt by Heaney who said that it would "wrench the rhythms" of his writing procedures to "start squaring up to contemporary events with more will than ways to deal with them" (*P*, 34). He referred to the Yeatsian example of writing in the context of a political and social crisis:

> I think that what he learned there was that you deal with public crisis not by accepting the terms of the public's crisis, but by making your own imagery and your own terrain take the colour of it, take the impressions of it. (Randall, 1979: 13)

This is precisely what Heaney does in his bog poems. Heaney told Broadbridge that he was always aware that his own

own inspiration sprang from "remembering" and he went on
to extrapolate this into a national fixation, seeing it as typical
of Irish people that they "looked back at their own history"
rather than forward towards the future. He went on to explore the ramifications of this: "The word 'remember' is a
potent word in Irish politics . . . Remember 1690 if you're an
Orangeman . . . Remember 1916 . . . if you are a republican"
(Broadbridge, 1977: 9).

Glob's book, with its photographs of Iron Age sacrificial
victims taken, almost complete, out of the bogs of Denmark,
has had an important influence on Heaney's work. It provides the metaphorical context which allows Heaney's personal digging into memory and what he sees as a national
Jungian excavation of memory to merge into a resonant
symbol wherein the bog people of ancient Europe become
symbols of the violence that is alive again in Northern Ireland. It is as if this resurrected sectarian hatred, which has
been buried under the seeming civilities of the Northern
Irish state, has now, like these bog people, come to the surface again in a chillingly lifelike manner. To see Glob's photographs of these Iron Age mummies is to be struck by their
wholeness and lack of decay. The bog has kept these bodies
whole, and in a parallel symbolic manner, the psychic memory of Heaney's own community, the Catholic, nationalist,
Irish "we" has done the same. This is also true of the Protestant community, but at this juncture in his career, Heaney
is writing very much from inside his own tradition. As he
puts it in the opening poem of *Wintering Out*:

Fodder

Or, as we said,
fother, I open
my arms for it
again. (*WO*, 13)

The fact that "we" say the word in a certain dialectal way presupposes that there is a "they" who say it differently. Northern Ireland has long been a place "where the ideological nature of linguistic choice is all-pervasive" (O'Brien, 1996: 146), and in these poems, Heaney is exploring the very nature of such choices. Having read Glob's book, and seen the photographs of these bog figures, especially the Tollund Man, Heaney felt that he knew he would "write a poem about it" (Haffenden, 1981: 57).

This poem would be a seminal one in Heaney's work, as it provided the answer to the central question which he set himself about the connection between the aesthetic and the political. Writing in "Feeling into Words", Heaney discusses his symbolic view of the conflict and sees this as, essentially, "a struggle between the cults and devotees of a god and a goddess", going on to exemplify these in terms of a struggle between "Mother Ireland" or "Kathleen Ni Houlihan" and "William of Orange" or "Edward Carson". For Heaney, these are the ideological figures and personifications with whom "the Irishmen and Ulstermen who do the killing" can identify. His view of the conflict as an essentially religious one may be, he agrees, remote from the political discussions and initiatives that are ongoing, but it is far from remote from the "bankrupt psychology and mythologies implicit in the terms Irish Catholic and Ulster Protestant" (*P*, 57).

Keeping in mind his attraction to the Yeatsian example of making his own imagery take the colour of the public crisis, Glob's book provides him with some of the symbols that are part of his own poetic technique. Glob argues in his book that a number of the Iron Age figures found buried in the bogs, including "the Tollund Man, whose head is now preserved near Aarhus in the museum at Silkeburg, were ritual sacrifices to the Mother Goddess" (*P*, 57). For Heaney, this notion of these people as bridegrooms to the goddess, as sacrifices which would ensure fertility in the

spring, was symbolic of an "archetypal pattern" and he tells
of how the photographs in the book fused with photographs
of contemporary atrocities in his mind.

There have been a number of critical readings of "The
Tollund Man", all agreeing on its importance in the Heaney
canon but all stressing different aspects of the poem. Elmer
Andrews sees the poem as enacting the pilgrimage that
Heaney suggests in the first line: "Some day I will go to Aarhus" (*WO*, 47), and as providing "endurance and continu-
ance" through its "techniques of assuagement". Andrews
makes a telling point about the tension between "allegiance
to 'our holy ground' with its sacrificial demands, and the
claims of individual values which react against the barbarism
of the sacrifice" (Andrews, 1988: 65–6). Corcoran also
stresses the religious aspect of the poem, comparing the
body of the Tollund Man with the "miraculously incorrupt
bodies of Catholic hagiology", and seeing this as a sign that
the Tollund Man may "be petitioned as a saint is". Corcoran
sees the hope, in the second section of the poem, that such
petitioning may make the recent dead germinate "as his kill-
ers hoped he would make their next season's crops germinate" (Corcoran, 1998: 35). Michael Molino stresses the role
of the speaker in the poem, and focuses, correctly in my
view, on the power of poetry to transform the Tollund Man
into a "transcendent power" who may be able to transform
"modern-day victims" into "sacrificial victims as well"
(Molino, 1994, 91).

All of these readings are correct, and form a powerful
response to this poem. However, keeping in mind the developmental and experiential context which we have been
discussing in terms of Heaney's notions of the bog and digging, I think that a focus on the structure of the poem, specifically its use of tenses, will allow us to achieve an even
more complete reading of this work. That the speaker of the
poem has never actually seen the Tollund Man has already

been made clear: the use of the future tense means that any actual encounter has not, as yet, taken place: hence "I will go . . . I will stand". However, the verbs representing the "I" of the poem in the second and third sections are not all in the future tense. Some are in the conditional tense: "I could risk . . . Something of his sad freedom . . . Should come to me", while the final stanza returns to the future:

> Out there in Jutland
> In the old man-killing parishes
> I will feel lost,
> Unhappy and at home. (*WO*, 48)

Heaney's response to the Tollund Man is essentially an intellectual one: he has read about him and seen his photograph in Glob's book. The background information provided by Glob, of the feminine religion personifying the earth as a mother, who required "new bridegrooms each winter to bed with her in her sacred place, in the bog, to ensure the renewal and fertility of the territory in the Spring" (*P*, 57), provides a context for Heaney's musings.

That these musings have a religious character is not, I think, in question. The shifting temporal focus of the poem bears out Bailey's point about the role of the past in the present. The first stanza is a complete sentence, describing how the poet "will go to Aarhus" to see the Tollund Man's "peat-brown head", while the second describes the actual unearthing of the bog figure, as "they dug him out". Interestingly, the "digging" theme is still at work here, as instead of the gravel, potatoes, "tall tops" or turf, what is now being unearthed is the very matter of the past. He goes on to describe both the exact physical state of the Tollund Man — his last meal of "winter seeds" still in his stomach — and the mythic and natural processes which have kept the corpse whole, like a "saint's kept body" — "She tightened her torc on him" and opened "her fen". It is as if his sacrifice for his people to the mother goddess has been rewarded with a kind of immortality. He has almost become like the bog itself, with his "peat-brown head", his eye-lids looking like "mild pods" and his skin coloured by the bog's "dark juices".

Heaney's Catholic sensibility would be quite responsive to the religious associations of pilgrimages to a saint's home, while the alliterative "Trove of the turfcutters' "is redolent of some of the Marian liturgy, especially "The Litany of the Blessed Virgin Mary". The image-pattern of the "stained face" of the head which "Reposes at Aarhus" recalls the stained-glass windows of many Catholic churches, and also, perhaps, the shroud of Turin, while the word "repose" is one used in the religious formula of praying for the "repose of the soul" of someone deceased. There is also the association of "the mild pods of his eye-lids" with a "subliminal reference to Jesus ('Gentle Jesus, meek and mild')" (Longley, 1986: 152). Hence, the way is paved in these submerged religious images of the opening section for the overtly religious dimension of the second section, a section wherein there is a temporal shift similar to those of "Digging" and "Bogland", but which differs in its use of the conditional tense.

When he says that he "*could* risk blasphemy" [*my italics*] and consecrate the cauldron bog, he means that it would be blasphemous to equate another deity, in this case the earth goddess, with the Christian God, who alone, according to Christian faith, has the power to grant eternal life. Yet such is the religious feeling inspired by both the Tollund Man and Glob's book that he wonders whether this preserved victim could "make germinate" the scattered bodies of "four young brothers" whose bodies were scattered along railway lines, having been the victims of sectarian murder in the 1920s.

Having posed the question, the final section of the poem features a split screen of two imagined journeys, as Heaney imagines his own future journey through Denmark on his way to see the Tollund Man's head in Aarhus, and compares this with the Tollund Man's last journey to his death by ritual sacrifice. He speaks of them both sharing a "sad freedom" and the poem ends with a further comparison, namely that in the "old man-killing parishes" Heaney will feel lost, unhappy and at home.

Perhaps the key to this poem is to be found in the images of turfcutters and digging, which point us back to that most seminal of Heaney poems. As we have noted earlier, "Digging" is located within the family home, and fixated on the patriarchal line of ancestry and occupation: grandfather and father are linked through digging and through the land: the poet, speaking in the poem, is the rupture in this sequence. Ironically, even as Heaney is attempting to build a connective bridge between his own activity of writing and the physical activity of digging, he is deconstructing the possibility of this happening as his form of "digging" will change the family tradition forever. In this sense, the image of the "curt cuts of an edge" through "living roots" which "awaken" in the poet's head is highly significant, as it is such cutting which will gradually separate the poet from his patriarchal line. At the same time, at a broader level, this image anticipates Heaney's gradual breaking free of the broader nationalist family: "braced and bound / Like brothers in a ring" (*FW*, 22), a process which is hinted at in these books, but more fully achieved in the later ones. The same point can be made of the initial simile "snug as a gun" which has no contextual placement in the poem, or indeed, in the first three books. The image of latent violence is, I would suggest, an unconscious realisation that he will break with his tradition.

In this context, "Digging" highlights a tension that is clear through his first books. He desires to write, in ways, out of his own experience, but the very fact that he is a writer, having gone to boarding school in Saint Columb's College and Queen's University means that he is no longer part of that rural familial life. It is interesting that, in talking about this poem, Heaney has used the terms "unconsciously" and "unselfconsciously" (Broadbridge, 1977: 6) as digging becomes a metaphor of the probing of the unconscious, unspoken aspects of his nationalist psyche throughout the early works. The same can be seen in "The Tollund Man", as he is drawn, at one level, to the religious notion of sacrifice as a redemptive action for the tribe, but at another, he sees both the Tollund Man, and the four young brothers as being dead, and whether the bodies are preserved or scattered, they remain dead. It is this realisation of both the attraction and ultimate futility of the tribal religion of place that is enacted by the movement of this poem.

Indeed, on closer reading, it becomes clear that the Tollund Man is now, in a sense, similar to the four brothers who have been decapitated in death, as he, too, has been decapitated: only his head is to be found at Aarhus. The connection between both is further solidified in the phrase "man-killing parishes" where the religious divisions of the land are described by the adjective "man-killing", a conceit that brings us back to Heaney's comments about the psychology of the people who "do the killing" in contemporary Northern Ireland.

It is highly attractive to believe that sacrifice can bring about renewal — it is a cornerstone of many religious faiths. However, what leaves the speaker in this poem "lost" and "unhappy" is the fact that, for both the bog victim and the four young brothers, there is no germination or rebirth. The nagging doubts about the bankruptcy of the psychological positions being adopted by the two communities in Northern Ireland are starting to deconstruct any sense of tribal bonding on Heaney's part. It is noticeable that in this poem the identification is not with the community, whether that of the Iron Age, of Ireland in the 1920s or of contemporary Ireland. He does not comment on the efficacy of the sacrifice, instead, he empathises with the victims, and with their suffering: his focus is on the "I" as opposed to the "we", even though the bog poems generally grant the validity of such territoriality. Whereas the Tollund Man can feel, Heaney imagines, a sense of "sad freedom" as his death is validated by his community, all Heaney can feel is lost and unhappy.

I would maintain that this sense of loss and unhappiness is caused in part by the realisation that notions of "home", of a territory that is sacred to a particular group, are often sanctioned by either a sacrifice from within the community or a scapegoating of the "other" outside. Heaney is only too aware of both types of violence in terms of his own "home". This sense of unease at sacrifices occasioned by tribal loyalties would surface again in his writing about the hunger strikes in Northern Ireland in the 1980s. What is being introduced here is a dissemination of meaning which traverses the classic Freudian boundary from *Heimlich* to *Unheimlich*. I would also suggest that this stance mirrored a growing unease at the actions of the PIRA, especially when they claimed to be the logical successors of the IRA and IRB who fought in 1916 and in the War of Independence. An interesting index of this unease was that, in 1966, the fiftieth anniversary of the Rising was celebrated with almost religious zeal in Ireland. Subsequent anniversaries, taking place in the shadow of the Northern Irish situation, were much more muted affairs.

This has to do with the interaction of the "I" with its different communities, and with the ongoing tension that such interaction brings to light. It is as if Heaney, while struggling to probe the psychic memory of his race, is also being pulled in a different direction. So, on the one hand, he speaks of a need to probe the memory of his own community, and of that community's relationship with land: "the landscape was sacramental, instinct with signs, implying a system of reality beyond the visible realities" (*P*, 132); while on the other, he is all too aware of the dangers of such an attraction between a tribe and a piece of land. The conclusion of "The Tollund Man" gives us a glimpse of the effect of this reality on Heaney the individual as opposed to Heaney as part of his community, the "slightly aggravated young Catholic male" (Deane, 1977: 66). While in one sense wishing to voice the concerns of his community, at another remove, he is unwilling to totally immerse himself emotionally in their sense of communality; hence the importance of the close of the poem as an indicator of how his thought will progress.

In *North*, the sense of communal, almost tribal belonging is stressed. Heaney has been accused of speaking the voice of his tribe in this book, of voicing "the actual substance of historical agony and dissolution, the tragedy of a people in a place: the Catholics of Northern Ireland" (Cruise O'Brien, 1975: 404). Edna Longley sees Heaney as avoiding the intersectarian issue, the "warfare *between* tribes", by concentrating on the Catholic psyche as "bound to immolation". She singles out the poem "Kinship" as defining the conflict in "astonishingly introverted Catholic and Nationalist terms" (Longley, 1986: 154). Ciarán Carson views the poems as in some way valorising the violence by placing it in a broad temporal and spatial pattern: it is as if he is saying that "suffering like this is natural; these things have always happened; they happened then, they happen now" (Carson, 1975: 184–5).

Blake Morrison also agrees that whether we "like it or not" such poetry grants "sectarian killing in Northern Ireland a historical respectability" which it is not normally granted in commentary on Northern Ireland. Like Carson, he feels that by placing contemporary violence in a broader context, "precedent becomes, if not a justification, than at least an 'explanation'" (Morrison, 1982: 68). As these critics make clear, the received reading of the first part of *North* is one of "tribal" writing. The Iron-Age bog victims are seen as

imaginative parallels to the victims of contemporary Northern Ireland. At another level, the "goddess" of the land, to
whom these votive offerings were made, is seen as analogous to the personified Ireland that is part of Irish cultural
nationalism. David Lloyd has made the point that the aes-
theticisation of Irish politics is brought about by a connection between "Irishness" and "Irish ground" and "Kathleen
Ni Houlihan, the motherland" (Lloyd, 1993: 17). The critics
cited above see *North* as part of this process.

These critical positions are valid up to a point. That
Heaney, in his first four books, is attempting to carve out
some form of poetic identity is clear. That he is so doing by
locating himself within the parameters of his tradition —
both familial and communal — is also clear. What we might
call the tribalisation of his personal "digging" and "bogland"
motifs achieves a climax in the bog poems of *North*; however, it is important that such poems be placed in context.
To see Heaney as someone almost intoxicated by the violence and carving out a role as the voice of his tribe is to
adopt an over-simplistic approach, at both the levels of biography and those of poetics. The reality is far more complex.

Heaney had spent a year at the University of California
at Berkeley and here imbibed the tail-end of the emancipa-
tory discourse of the 1960s. As he put it, the atmosphere at
Berkeley was "politicised and minorities like the Chicanos
and Blacks were demanding their say". He saw that there
was a close connection between this consciousness-raising in
America and the "political and cultural assertions being
made at that time by the minority in the north of Ireland"
(Randall, 1979: 19–20). By further extending his digging and
bog motifs, he saw that he had a sufficiently agile symbolic
structure which could take the weight of this voicing of minority identity. Thus, in *North*, the bog poems are arranged
in order to create a layered presentation of this mythic form
of identity.

The metrical and verbal forms of *Wintering Out* and *North* were also affected by his sojourn in America, with the short, four-stress line allowing a looser form of expression, while also providing a formal unity to the first part of each book. The division of each book into two parts, one broadly mythic in theme and tone, the other dealing with issues of a more contemporary nature, enacts the different levels of identity that were the focus of Heaney's attention. At one level, he was part of his community, his selfhood being formed by the watermarks of tradition and group, and the opening sections probe the nature of this communal aspect of the self. The second parts of the books look, more specifically in *North*, at the contemporary watermarks of the anonymities, and how they affect life in Northern Ireland where "Men die at hand" (*N*, 58), and where the voice of sanity attempts to distance itself from the acts of violence being perpetrated in the name of community. However, it is to Part I of *North* that we first turn in order to examine the development of the seminal trope of digging into the bog, as symbolic of examining the visceral roots of identity.

This act of unearthing the past is the subject of "Come to the Bower", itself the title of an Irish folk song, which recounts the act of uncovering "the dark-bowered queen" by "hand". This is an image which, as Patricia Coughlin, who has provided a seminal feminist critique of Heaney's work, notes, "combines the traditional topos of disrobing with the richly sensuous apprehension of the landscape which is one of Heaney's most characteristic features" (Coughlin, 1997: 194). The imagery and narrative are suffused with a strong sexual subtext, as the sensory aspects of the act, the hand being "touched" by sweetbriar before going on to "unpin" the queen, and to "unwrap skins" are dwelt upon. This chain is reinforced by the phallic imagery of "sharpened willow" which "Withdraws gently" out of "the black maw / Of the peat", and the added image of spring water which starts "to rise around her". The culmination of this sexual image chain is the final reaching of the "bullion" of her "Venus bone" (*N*, 31). This sexual development of the basic digging motif is a further extension of the scope of this image. I would suggest that Heaney is using the image in a broadly Freudian sense, to mean a form of bodily (or somatic) pleasure, a pleasure that comes from the acceptance of the bonds of community and from a sense of unity. The violence that is always implicated in such cultural fusion is implied in the sense of rape and violation that underpins this sexual strain of imagery.

In the next poem, "Bog Queen", the thematic process is similar but the perspective is completely altered. Thus far, in all of the artesian poems which we have examined, the perspective has been that of the "digger", the searcher within the present for some form of memory of the past, someone who is metaphorically chewing "the cud of memory" (*N*, 17). In this poem, however, it is one of the unearthed objects which speaks, the personified "Bog Queen" herself who depicts her history and her sense of waiting to be unearthed, and, symbolically, to be brought back to some form of life in the poem. The repeated "I lay waiting" stresses the fact that, though dead, there is some form of sentience still at work in the consciousness of the bog queen; she remains conscious of all of the processes of decay even as she undergoes them: the "seeps of winter / digested me". Her brain is seen as "darkening", and compared to a "jar of spawn" which is "fermenting underground" (*N*, 32). The constant use of the pronoun "my" to explain the processes of nature underlines the consciousness of the speaker, and the fact that she retains some form of life. The length of time she has been "waiting" is beautifully caught by the use of the unusual verb which describes how the "phoenician stitchwork / retted" on on her breasts' "soft moraines" (*N*, 33). This verb, which derives from the Middle English *roten*, meaning "to soften by soaking in water or by exposure to moisture to encourage partial rotting", captures the gradual rotting of both the body and the clothing which covered that body. The sheer length of time involved in this process is indicated by the use of "moraines" to describe the queen's breasts, as this word refers to an area or bank of debris that a glacier or ice sheet has carried down and deposited.

The almost complete transformation from human to natural object that is undergone by the bog queen seems to indicate a direction in the poem which will see her totally subsumed by the land: "the seeps of winter / digested me" (*N*, 32). However, in the closing stanza and a half, the imagery of decomposition is inverted, and death becomes metamorphosised into a rebirth:

> The plait of my hair,
> a slimy birth-chord
> of bog, had been cut
>
> and I rose from the dark,
> hacked bone, skull-ware. (*N*, 34)

Here, the sentience of memory is symbolised in this image of death being transformed into rebirth. This is possibly his most graphic figuring of the idea of memory as having a life of its own, and it complements the previous poem, "Come to the Bower". There, the "I" of the poem went searching for "the dark-bowered queen" while here, it is the self-same queen who speaks: she is sentient, aware and "waiting" for this very moment when she can be unveiled and reborn. It is this latent power of memory to incubate the wrongs of the past and to keep them alive in the minds of a community that is the subject of these poems. The imagery of violation, conveyed by the verbs "barbered / and stripped" (*N*, 33), is a further link in the image chain which connects violence and pain with this process of memory as a form of communal incubation.

It is as if sectarian hatred has remained dormant for years and, just when it seemed dead, it emerged from the depths of the communal or tribal psychic ground to repeat the "murderous" encounters of the past in the present. This is the reality of the "germination" that can occur from the tribal religious sacrifice of "The Tollund Man", and from the seeds of revolution that were the subject of "Requiem for the Croppies". The bog queen, alive and "skull-ware", a term which has meanings ranging from "guarded" to "protected" to "defensive" to "cunning" to "conscious", symbolises the reality of the irruption of the past onto the present. It is a harbinger of violence and of a sense of tribal bonding which experiences the erotic pleasures of identification and community. Heaney has stressed the intimate attractiveness of such a position of tribal immanence in these poems, perhaps too well, in the light of the criticism which they have received. He is all too aware that such sectarian nationalistic positions, while logically difficult to defend, achieve their ends through aesthetic, sexual and cultural means.

This is at the core of "The Grauballe Man", wherein the dead figure is described in intimate detail, as if he were a work of art in himself. In this poem, there are very few verbs denoting physical contact; instead, the poem functions like a moving camera, focusing on different aspects of the physical appearance of the bog figure. Here, he functions as an image, as an icon (Corcoran, 1998: 71), and Heaney has brought to the fore the crucial importance of the image or icon in the discourse of identity and nationalism. It is the bog figure as image that preoccupies this poem: he is described in terms of an aesthetic object, an object which is intimately connected with the natural processes. Through simile and metaphor, he is compared to "bog oak", "a basalt egg", "swan's foot", a "wet swamp root", a "mussel" and "an eel" (*N*, 35), with the overall effect being to dehumanise him by

making him seem almost a part of nature. Heaney asks this
rhetorical question:

> Who will say "corpse"
> to his vivid cast?
> Who will say "body"
> to his opaque repose? (*N*, 36)

Thomas Docherty sees this stanza as asking: "is history dead,
a thing of the past; or is it alive, vivid, a presence of the past"
(Docherty, 1991: 70). These were the very questions that
Irish people, north and south, were asking as sectarian violence flared in the streets of Northern Ireland. The unquestioned assumptions of nationalist Ireland, that the 1916 Rising was a good thing, that the IRA had the right to bear arms
in the name of the Irish people, and that there was a historical imperative that saw a "United Ireland" as its *telos* were
coming into question, though very gradually. Having called
the status of the bog figure into question, Heaney goes on to
repeat the same death-resurrection trope that we saw in
"Bog Queen" as the Grauballe Man's hair is compared, again
in simile, to a "foetus", and later, to a "forceps baby". The
idea that this man's death, a death caused by a "slashed
throat", has somehow been arrested, and that he now becomes the ultimate image of a rebirth, is a classic example of
the power of the aesthetic to persuade an audience that
death for the tribe can have a salvific purpose. This is why
much of *North* has been read as justifying, or glorifying, such
violence.

   However, in keeping with that critical trend which we
have been tracing through these poems, Heaney also creates
a counter-movement, a movement in this case which occurs
over the long sentence that is the final four stanzas of the
poem. He tells of how he first saw the Grauballe Man's
"twisted face" in a photograph, but that now he is "per-

fected in my memory". The movement from the external to
the internal that structurally underpinned so much of
Heaney's artesian imagery is evident here again, as this ancient figure, dug "out of the peat" is balanced in the poet's
memory: "hung in the scales / with beauty and atrocity". On
one side of this particular scale is the Dying Gaul (a sculp-
ture from the third century B.C. depicting a dying Celtic
warrior, with matted hair, lying on his shield, wounded, and
awaiting death, now to be found in the Capitoline museum
in Rome), and on the other:

> the actual weight
> of each hooded victim,
> slashed and dumped. (*N*, 36)

Here, the poem, which seemed to be endorsing an aesthetic
approach to this figure, now suddenly broaches the contrast
between an actual piece of art, the Dying Gaul, an imaginative creation, and the Grauballe Man, a victim of tribal sacrifice, killed in a most unpleasant manner. Factually, Glob
noted that the "cut ran . . . practically from ear to ear, so
deep that the gullet was completely severed" (Glob, 1969:
48).

The word that tips the balance here is the adjective "actual" which stresses the reality of lifting the dead weight of
hooded victims, after they were "slashed". Whether these
victims are Iron Age figures or contemporary victims of
Northern Irish violence is not specified, but I would suggest
that he is referring to contemporary figures, and I would
also feel that he is, once again, foregrounding the victim and
the reality of death, as opposed to some form of mythic religious dimension. Again, there was a societal parallel as the
images of the victims of PIRA and loyalist bombings and
shootings began to register with television audiences, and
people began to wonder whether political ideology of either

sort was worth such suffering. This reading is underscored by the next bog poem, "Punishment", a poem for which Heaney has been severely criticised for seeming to justify the nationalist community's attempts at punishing young Catholic girls who dated British soldiers. Once again, the past–present dialectic is the structural and thematic kernel of the poem, as the speaker empathically feels "the wind / on her naked front", a reference to the Windeby girl, who was punished for adultery in Iron Age Germany by being bound, tied to a "weighing stone" and drowned.

The poem again utilises the external–internal movement as the initial five-and-a-half stanzas are purely descriptive, addressing the reader implicitly, and talking about the girl in the third person. However at the exact centre of the poem, the mode of address changes, as now he speaks directly to the "Little adulteress" in apostrophe, and tells, in the past tense, how she looked before "they punished you" (N, 38). His involvement becomes all the more intense, as he appears to succumb to the erotica of her "nipples", her "naked front" (N, 37) and her "flaxen" hair, stating, "I almost love you". But this love is qualified by the admission that he, too, would have "cast the stones of silence", as in the present, he has "stood dumb" while women in analogous situations, Catholic women who have been intimate with British soldiers, have been similarly punished: "your betraying sisters / cauled in tar, / wept by the railings". This refers to a practice of tying young girls so accused to railings, shaving parts of their hair and covering them in tar.

Heaney, noting the comparison, and analysing his feelings of empathy for the Windeby girl, is honest enough to locate the parallel, and even more honestly realises that while he affects horror at the death of the "Little adulteress", he has been aware of similar punishments, and in the closing stanza he explains the reasons for his inaction, seeing himself as someone:

who would connive
in civilized outrage
yet understand the exact
and tribal, intimate revenge. (*N*, 38)

Here, Heaney appears to be voicing the atavisms of his tribe. As Cruise O'Brien puts it, "It is the word 'exact' that hurts most" (Cruise O'Brien, 1975: 404), as, like "actual" in the previous poem, it intrudes a reality on the poetic and aesthetic form that gives it a connection with the actual suffering that is an ongoing facet of the Northern Irish violence. At a rational and intellectual level, Heaney, as an educated man, would express "civilized outrage" at such barbaric treatment of people in the twentieth century; however, at a traditional and visceral level, he does understand why "his" community feels the need to act in such a manner. The Provisional IRA, the people carrying out such a "punishment", see themselves as the defenders of the Catholic community, and any action that would give aid or comfort to the enemy, is deemed as being in need of "punishment". It is part of the strength of these poems that in them, Heaney allows that visceral aspect of his nationalist, Catholic identity to speak out. Such atavisms and sectarian prejudices seldom get an airing in the politically correct world of television interviews and newspaper articles. However, it is precisely such atavistic emotions that are the motive forces of the people who, in Heaney's words, "do the killing" (*P*, 57). As he put in an interview, "the problem with the IRA is that you're dealing with theology rather than politics" (Farndale, 2001: 10), and it is this theological aspect of the Catholic republican psyche that is so well enunciated in this book. Belief that one is acting for the good of one's tribe is a powerful force, as it allows all morality to be bypassed for the good of that tribe. Here he reflects an ambivalence towards IRA violence that has been a factor in the ongoing tacit support which they have received.

This belief is the source of the final irony of this poem, which is to be found in the symmetry of the initial word of the title and the closing word of the poem. The very notion of "punishment" implies a hierarchical structure in the service of some form of law: one is punished for transgressing some rule or regulation. The OED suggests that the word implies some "offence" or "misconduct", and there is an element of justice also implied in the use of the word. In the present context, Heaney would seem to be according nationalist Catholic violence against young women the status of a quasi-legal imposition of a penalty against misconduct. However, in that ongoing pattern of undercutting the seeming certainties of earlier parts of a poem in the latter sections, he changes the tenor of the whole discussion with his use of the last word "revenge". Here the legality or morality of the tribal position is undercut: it is not justice, but a form of revenge against those who have gone outside the tribe that is at work here. This word, allied to the readings of the other bog poems, undercuts any over-simplistic reading of these as simply voicing the anger of the tribe from within. Heaney "understands" such anger, but he neither sanctions nor condones it.

In "Kinship", he foregrounds that initial image of unearthing the past, the spade, seeing it in completely symbolic terms:

> I found a turf-spade
> hidden under bracken,
> laid flat, and overgrown
> with a green fog. (N, 42)

In this return to his poetic and historical origins, the spade again becomes the lever which unearths the past. In "Digging", it was the familial past; here, it is the symbolic past, as what is unearthed in this poem is the nationalist memory of wrongs done as he stands at the "edge of centuries / facing a goddess" (*N*, 42). Here, the sexual imperative towards a bond with this tribal memory is captured in the phallic imagery of the spade penetrating "the soft lips of growth", the "shaft wettish" and "upright" (*N*, 42). It is also significant that the adjective "green" is used, a colour which signifies republicanism in contradistinction to the orange of unionism.

Heaney tells us of his visceral attraction to this sense of his tradition, noting how he "grew" out of this sense of the past as sacred, comparing himself in simile to a "weeping willow" which was inclined to "the appetites of gravity" (*N*, 43). This leads to the final section of the poem, where he defines himself as part of a tribal identity, making his grove on an old crannog (an altar of stones) in honour of "Our mother ground", and asking Tacitus to "report us fairly", as he goes on to describe how "we slaughter / for the common good" and "shave the heads" of the notorious (*N*, 45). These lines, a classic example of "memory incubating the spilled blood" (*N*, 20), would seem to copper-fasten the view of Heaney as the voice of his tribe; however, as in the previous poems, there is a more complicated perspective at work. In section IV of the poem, having described the "appetites of gravity", he tells how "I grew out of all this", a phrase which is highly ambiguous, as it can mean that he traces his roots back to this visceral sense of territorial loyalty, or, significantly, that he has outgrown this past sense of loyalty. There is the sense that the present poet is looking back at an earlier incarnation of himself. He is writing at a time when people were joining paramilitary organisations on both sides of the border, and when feelings were running high in terms of support for the PIRA in nationalist circles. However, there were also questions being raised about the givens of nationalism, notably by Conor Cruise O'Brien and John A. Murphy, who were attempting to bring a different perspective to bear on these issues.

Crucially, in terms of such perspective, Tacitus, as Roman historian, never came to Ireland; nor did the Romans. This section is highly imaginative as opposed to historical; Tacitus represents an external perspective which Heaney is beginning to deem necessary. In fact, what Heaney is providing here is an imagined Ireland, an Ireland of the mind, an Ireland incarnated from within the nationalist *mythos*, an Ireland which is constructed from images, symbols and partial readings of history from within the tribal tradition of Catholic republican nationalism. The image of the territory as a goddess who is worshipped by an "us" also helps to define the very nature of that "us". It is real, relevant but ultimately one-dimensional. It is part of the enabling socio-cultural tradition from which Heaney has come, but it is also a limiting factor on his growth as an individual, especially one who is now living in a mixed, middle-class area where the old tribalisms have been ameliorated by the voices of education and learning.

The Heaney who "grew out of all this" is to be found in the more contemporary second section, where the complexities of living in a middle-class area, and a middle-class society with the liberal unionist side by side with the "liberal papist", both speaking in what he calls "the voice of sanity" (*N*, 58). Here, far from the tribal certainty and warmth, we see the complexities of speaking to those of the other tradition: "expertly civil tongued with civil neighbours", speaking the "sanctioned, old, elaborate retorts" (*N*, 57), while harbouring a desire to "lure the tribal shoals to epigram / And order" (*N*, 59). The complex speaker of "Whatever You Say Say Nothing" and "Exposure" seems very removed from the atavistic certainty of slaughtering for the common good, and understanding the intimate nature of revenge. In "Singing School", he speaks of other forces which shaped the person he was to become: "Saint Columb's College" in Derry, for example, which helped him to "gaze into new worlds" (*N*, 63). It was this educative process that would further sunder those roots, and would allow Heaney to move outside of the sacral territory of the bog poems, and on to "Belfast and Berkeley" (*N*, 63). It was these voices of education that would give him the confidence to write poetry which would ultimately transform both the givens of his own identity, and that of Ulster: "Ulster was British, but with no rights on / The English lyric" (*N*, 65).

The sense of physical movement outward from his own home, both real and psychic, is clear in section four of "Singing School", entitled "Summer 1969". This summer was the flashpoint around which the antagonism between nationalist and unionist traditions in Northern Ireland was to ignite. The opening lines of this poem demonstrate another Ireland of the mind in Heaney's work, Ireland far from the immanence and tribalism of "Kinship", as when the police were assisting the mob which was shooting into the Falls Road, in Belfast, Heaney was suffering only "the bullying sun of Madrid" (*N*, 69). In this poem, there is a sense of coming full circle in the repeated image of "flax" in two similes in the opening section: "stinks from the fishmarket / Rose like the reek of a flax-dam" and the "patent leather of the Guardia Civil" which gleamed "like fish-bellies in flax-poisoned waters" (*N*, 69). This image of flax was central to the title poem of his first collection *Death of a Naturalist*: "All year the flax-dam festered in the heart / Of the townland . . . Flax had rotted there" (*DON*, 15). In this poem, there is a dawning of awareness that nature has an existence of its own, outside the cosy world of the "daddy frog" and the "mammy frog". The invasion of the flax-dam by the "angry frogs" at the end of the poem symbolises a Freudian return of the repressed, as nature claims its right to exist without interference. In ways, this poem anticipates the poems of "Singing

School" as here, too, the simplicities of a one-sided perspective are jettisoned and a more comprehensive if less comfortable viewpoint is developed. The repeated mention of
flax harks back to this poem, and raises the possibility that
"Singing School" implies the "death of a nationalist"!

In "Summer 1969", the movement away from the territory has led to a more complicated attitude on the part of
Heaney, as he proceeds to question the role of the artist in
the face of such political and social violence. Should he heed
the advice of a friend and "Go back" and "try to touch the
people", or should he emulate Lorca or Goya? In this poem,
there is a sense that art will always be a mediating factor,
not actually part of "the real thing" (*N*, 69), and this is an
alternative position to the "voice of the tribe" that we saw
in the bog poems. There is already a sense that an alternative position is being developed in this sequence, whose title
itself is interesting in this regard. The title is taken from
Yeats's poem "Sailing to Byzantium" where Yeats, desiring
to emulate the artistic unity and coherence of the Byzantine
civilisation, makes the point that "Nor is there singing school
but studying / Monuments of its own magnificence" (Yeats,
1979: 217). The point however is that art very often thrives
through its interaction with other forms of art and, in
"Summer 1969", it is the type of art that Heaney should be
creating that is troubling him. Indeed, it is while ostensibly
describing the work of Goya that he comes up with an abid-
ing reference to the two communities in Northern Ireland
as a "holmgang" (duel to the death) where two "berserks"
fight to the death "greaved in a bog, and sinking" (*N*, 70).

The distance from both positions is highly significant
here. It is probably the first time that he has used the term
"bog" without a loaded, personal and political significance. It
is as if the physical distance from Ireland is paralleled by a
metaphysical distance from the tribal position. Through art,
he can create an alternative Ireland of the mind. The penul-

timate section, entitled "Fosterage", is dedicated to Michael McLaverty, the principal of St Thomas's Intermediate School in Ballymurphy, where Heaney worked as a student teacher. McLaverty was a writer himself, and clearly exerted an important influence on Heaney. This implicit point is made explicit through the quotation "Description is revelation", a quote attributed to McLaverty, who also gives Heaney some advice that will be paralleled by another mentor in *Station Island*, telling him to "Listen. Go your own way. / Do your own work" (*N*, 71).

In this context, the poem is hopeful in the sense that Vaclav Havel has used the term. Heaney writes of this in an essay about the IRA truce entitled "Cessation 1994". He speaks of Havel's very specific definition of hope, which is not specifically connected to optimism. For Havel, hope is "not the expectation that things will turn out successfully but the conviction that something is worth waiting for, however it turns out" (*FK*, 47). It is a hope based on the ameliorative power of the individual consciousness in a situation in need of amelioration. It is this focus on the self, on the "I", and on the transformative power of listening and working on the givens that construct that "I" that will concern us in the second chapter.

Chapter Two

Door into the Light

> I remember writing a letter to Brian Friel just after *North* was published, saying I no longer wanted a door into the dark — I want a door into the light. And I suppose as a natural corollary or antithesis to the surrender, to surrendering one's imagination to something as embracing as myth or landscape, I really wanted to come back to be able to use the first person singular to mean *me* and my lifetime. (Randall, 1979: 20)

Interestingly, this aspect of Heaney's development as a poet can actually be seen to have preceded *Field Work*. We have traced what has been termed his artesian imagination through personal, communal and eventually mythic and psychic memory in the opening chapter. We have made the point that the vector of his poetic gaze was invariably in an inward, downward and metaphorically backward direction as he sought a sense of individual definition within his familial and social communities: "my quest for definition, while it may lead backward, is conducted in the living speech of the landscape I was born into" (*P*, 36–7). This definition, as we have seen, is largely that of his community, and the temporal perspective is very much that of mythological time.

We have already examined the different perspective of "Singing School", at the close of *North*. In the closing poem of this sequence, however, we find the speaking "I" of the poem located very much in contemporary time: "It is December in Wicklow". This very direct opening allows us to situate the poem in Heaney's Glanmore period. He and his wife moved their family to Glanmore, to a small cottage owned by Anne Saddlemeyer (the dedicatee of the "Glanmore Sonnets" in *Field Work*), and attempted to focus on the contemporary and the personal. Heaney has made a number of comments on the importance of this period of his life in terms of his poetic development. He sees this period as "fundamental to securing my sense of myself as a poet" (Murphy, 2000b: 87). He had already said that, after *North*, he wanted to "pitch the voice out" (Randall, 1979: 16), and this process was to become overt in *Field Work* where he tells of how he wanted "to be able to use the first person singular to mean *me* and my lifetime" [*italics original*] (Randall, 1979: 20). This is a major change of perspective when we think of the "I" of the bog poems, who was unpinning a symbolic figure, and the "I" of "Kinship" and "Punishment" who was voicing the atavisms of his tribe. The title of *Field Work* resonates with levels of meaning, all of which point towards the present and future of Heaney's own life at this time. It can refer to work carried out in the natural environment by a surveyor, collector of scientific data, or sociologist, indicating that this book will be a collection of images and thoughts which can later contribute to a theoretical structure. A further level of meaning is to be found in the contextual placement of this term: given his domicile in rural County Wicklow, Heaney is now "working" on his current environment: his work, his writing, will be surrounded, not in archaeological digs or bogs, but in fields.

In "Exposure" (from *North*), situated temporally and spatially outside the territory of Northern Ireland, the "I" of the poem is definitely referring to Heaney's contemporary situation. The title refers to an exposure to the complexities of the present as opposed to the mythic certainties of the earlier part of *North*. The perspective in this poem is upward as opposed to downward, as he looks for a "comet" that should be "visible at sunset". In terms of the voice of the tribe, that imagined Ireland already seems to be at a distance from this poem, as he walks through damp leaves:

> Imagining a hero
> On some muddy compound,
> His gift like a slingstone
> Whirled for the desperate. (*N*, 72)

There is already a sense of separation between the voice of the poem and this imagined "hero", whose art is a form of weapon in defence of his communal identity.

The exposure in question leads to questions which serve to complicate the stance of the poet with respect to his role: "How did I end up like this?" (*N*, 72), and he goes on to examine the "weighing and weighing" of his "responsible *tristia*" (*N*, 73). He asks for whom he is writing, and it is here that the curt cuts of an edge sunder him from the sense of speaking from within the sacred home of the tribe, as the answer to the question is far from comforting or certain: "For what? For the ear? For the people? / For what is said behind-backs" (*N*, 73). He exposes himself, and the givens of his tradition, to a searching critique, leading him to define himself negatively as "neither internee nor informer" — as someone who is neither so committed to nationalism that he is likely to be interned, nor as someone who is so removed from its ideology that he would inform on militant republicans.

This alliterative phrase encapsulates a very real dilemma in the Ireland of the 1970s. From an unthought sense of

common cause with the nationalist population of Northern
Ireland, a gradual sense of historical revisionism began to
take hold of the national mindset. From an initially defensive
role, the campaign of the Provisional IRA took on an offen-
sive dimension, with various groups being deemed "legitimate targets". Some of the bombings, with the resultant loss
of life, caused a number of people to seriously question their
allegiance to "republicanism". For example, in the light of the
death of seven people in a car bomb in Donegal Street,
Belfast in March 1972, or the deaths of a further eight people in car bombs on 21 July of the same year, or the nine
people killed in an explosion at Claudy, County Derry later
in the same month, it became harder for people to sympathise with their aims or to understand the undoubtedly reac-
tive nature of their foundation and original inception. Innocent civilians, killed because bomb warnings were either in-
accurate or badly timed, hardly seemed to be the romantic
road to the "fourth green field" or "a nation once again", to
use phrases from two nationalist folk ballads.

This had the additional effect of causing intellectuals and
the media to interrogate many of the foundational myths of
the state, including the Easter Rising of 1916, a rising with
which the Provisionals made common cause in terms of the
use of political violence without any democratic mandate.
Heaney's increasingly individual questioning of the simplistic
acceptance that nationalists should, by definition, support the
"armed struggle", can be seen in the progression of attitude
across the books in this section. I would suggest that this parallels a similar process of questioning in society at large, and
Heaney's writing played no small part in this complication of
response to the issues of political violence and identity.

This process of questioning had long-term political ramifications. The constitution of the Republic of Ireland, enacted in 1937, had always laid claim to the whole island of
Ireland (it wasn't until the Good Friday Agreement of April

1998 that this claim was removed from the constitution by a referendum margin of 94 per cent). Heaney's notion of "feeling every wind that blows" captures this sense of doubt and uncertainty about the core values of Irish society and its past that had been initiated by the republican campaign of violence. In "Exposure", there is no discourse of loyalty to the past or to a personified notion of that past. Significantly, the bog is demythologised succinctly by being called a "muddy compound". Here there is no sense of the communal: the voice is individual and full of questions and doubts. The poem is redolent of an attitude which will be given expression in *Station Island*, in a quotation from Czeslaw Miłosz's "Native Realm":

> *I was stretched between contemplation*
> *of a motionless point*
> *and the command to participate*
> *actively in history.* [*italics original*] (*SI*, 16)

The doubts and questions as to the role of art in the processes of history, and more specifically, the "responsible" role that Heaney should adopt in terms of Northern Ireland, now that he is exiled from it, are integral to *Field Work*, and specifically to the elegies in that book. Heaney tells of how the structure of *Field Work* has been shaped by this desire to voice his contemporary experience, with all of its doubts and uncertainties:

> The activity of writing originates very, very far down,
> and is affected by everything in your life, and it *should*
> affect everything in your life. I found in Glanmore . . .
> that you had to be really coherent, and you had to
> be in earnest. [*italics original*] (Haffenden, 1981: 69)

Writing about the deaths of real, contemporary people allowed Heaney to discuss how death can affect the individual who has been exposed to it. Without the communal security blanket of tribal bonding, such violent deaths have a chilling effect on the individual. "The Strand at Lough Beg" refers to Colum McCartney, "a second cousin" of Heaney's who was "shot arbitrarily" as he was "coming home from a football match in Dublin" (Randall, 1979: 21). In this poem, Heaney attempts to imagine how death came to McCartney, positing either a "faked road block" and "the cold-nosed gun" or else "in your driving mirror, tailing headlights" of a car which pulled out "suddenly and flagged you down" (*FW*, 17). At the end of the poem, Heaney imagines himself washing the dead body with "handfuls of dew", and dabbing it "clean with moss" before plaiting "Green scapulars to wear over your shroud" with rushes that grow near Lough Beg (*FW*, 18). As Lloyd puts it, this poem characterises the speaker's actions as "ritualistic, reproducing man's ancient and ongoing need to cleanse, anoint, mourn and honour the dead" (Lloyd, 1981: 88). Here, the role of art is to comfort and assuage the death of an individual: the notion of understanding that this death may be part of some historical process is eschewed in favour of a more personal, exposed feeling of sorrow and pity. I would argue that this process parallels the transformation of attitudes of people in Ireland as a whole to the ongoing violence in Northern Ireland.

"A Postcard from North Antrim" concerns a man named Sean Armstrong who Heaney had known at Queens, and who had been part of the "commune pot-smoking generation" in Sausalito, before coming back to Belfast "to get involved in social work and worked at children's playgrounds". He was "shot by some unknown youth" (Randall, 1979: 21). Here again, the reaction to the violence is personal and contemporary as opposed to mythic. The history and personality depicted in this poem is that of Armstrong, in his "gallowglass's beard" swinging on the "*Carrick-a-Rede Rope Bridge*". This image, deepened by the account of his "Ethnically furnished" houseboat, is made contemporary in the two metaphors: "Drop-out on a come-back" and prince of "no-man's land". His return to Belfast is terminated when his "candid forehead" stopped a "pointblank teatime bullet" (*FW*, 19). It is the adjective "teatime" that encapsulates the "normality" of violent death in Northern Ireland in the 1970s. Like McCartney, Armstrong was apolitical, an innocent victim, who is painted in Heaney's memory as singer of songs, splasher of wine, and the provider of the "floor" where Heaney put his arm around Marie's shoulder for the "first time". His idea of political involvement was a "local, hoped for, unfound commune", and his voice was redolent of notions of an older "independent, rattling, non-transcendent" notion of Ulster, what is termed "old decency" (*FW*, 20).

The third elegy, "Casualty", describes a fisherman, Louis O'Neill, who used to come to Heaney's father-in-law's public house in County Tyrone. He was killed in an explosion "in a curfew" imposed by the Provisional IRA three nights after "they shot dead / the thirteen men in Derry" (*FW*, 22). The background to "Bloody Sunday" was that on Sunday 30 January 1972, at approximately 4.10 p.m., soldiers of the Support Company of the 1st Battalion Parachute Regiment opened fire on the marchers in the Rossville Street area. By about 4.40 p.m., the shooting had ended, with 13 people dead and a further 13 injured from gunshots. Nationalist opinion was outraged, and the symbolic import of the 13 funerals coming out of the "packed cathedral" in Derry is highlighted by Heaney. In "Casualty", these funerals are described in terms of the common funeral of "Funeral Rites" from *North*:

> The common funeral
> Unrolled its swaddling band,
> Lapping, tightening
> Till we were braced and bound
> Like brothers in a ring. (*FW*, 22)

The sense of communal bonding that was so evident in the wake of Bloody Sunday is precisely that which Heaney spoke of in *North* when he used the phrase "understand the exact / and tribal, intimate revenge" in "Punishment"; and also when he asked Tacitus to report fairly "how we slaughter / for the common good" in "Kinship".

However, in this poem, while there is sympathy with the commonality of the bond, there is also sympathy with the solitary curfew breaker: "but he would not be held / At home by his own crowd" (*FW*, 22). Whereas in *North*, the victims were seen as part of the larger historical and mythic pattern, here, Louis O'Neill is seen as a more enigmatic figure, and the perspective of the speaker of the poem is similarly enigmatic:

> How culpable was he
> That last night when he broke
> Our tribe's complicity? (*FW*, 23)

It is a question that is not answered in this poem; however, I would argue that it is a question which is not even asked in the mythic poems of *North*. His funeral is contrasted with that of the 13 dead, with "quiet walkers" and "sideways talkers". It is at the end of the poem that the relevance of Louis O'Neill is suggested, as Heaney remembers the "freedom" he tasted with him. O'Neill becomes a paradigm of Heaney the poet, but interestingly the "proper haunt" of such freedom is defined as "Somewhere, well out, beyond . . ." (*FW*, 24). At the close of the poem, it is the dead individual, as opposed to those dead from the tribe, that is of lasting influence on Heaney, who asks the "Dawn-sniffing revenant" to "Question me again" (*FW*, 24). This image anticipates a resonant line from "Tollund" in *The Spirit Level* where he describes himself as being "at home beyond the tribe" (*SL*, 69).

In the detail of these elegies, there is no trace of any form of "understanding" of the killings, or of their being in any way for "the common good". There is a vastly different perspective involved here, as the mythic notion of Ireland's past that we saw in the bog poems has been replaced by a more humane concern with the plight of individuals. The ongoing reality of the violence in Northern Ireland had dampened any sense of romance that may have accompanied the beginnings of the "troubles". It is this questioning of the validity of the tribal bond that is the seminal trope of these books. What was voiced as almost a given in *North* has now become something which needs to be interrogated. For Emmanuel Levinas, one of the central imperatives of the artist is that "he needs to interpret his myths himself" (Levinas, 1989: 143), and this is precisely the process undertaken by Heaney here.

In "Triptych", earlier in *Field Work*, he describes the ongoing violence in terms that are both contemporary and distant from its source. Written after the murder of Sir Christopher Ewart-Biggs, the British Ambassador to Ireland, by the Provisional IRA on 21 July 1976, the poem points to the connection between two "young men with rifles on a hill" and the "unquiet founders", stressing the putative connection between the contemporary IRA and the original figures from 1916, and the later War of Independence, a connection validated by memory: "as if our memory hatched them" (*FW*, 12). The poem is no longer emphatic in its use of "we", with lines such as "Who's sorry for our trouble?" (*FW*, 12) and "Our island is full of comfortless noises" (*FW*, 13). This connection between contemporary and historical republicanism was being made more frequently in the media, with the assassination of Ewart-Biggs causing widespread revulsion in the Republic of Ireland. While there may still be a "bracing" aura to violence, there is a gradual sense that such action is also "profane", a position gestured to by this poem (*FW*, 12).

In *Field Work*, there is also a change in the type of stan-
zaic structure and rhythm that is used. Structurally, the poems of *Wintering Out* and *North* enacted the artesian imagination which was thematically at work in them: "I was burrow-
ing inwards, and those thin small quatrain poems, they're
kind of drills or augers for turning in and they are narrow
and long and deep" (Randall, 1979: 16). In *Field Work*, he was
setting out to speak more to a contemporary audience than
to a mythic one, so he used different rhythms: "the rhythmic
contract of meter and iambic pentameter and long line implies audience" (Randall, 1979: 16). There is certainly a more
self-conscious sense of the structure of the line and of ex-
perimentation with different poetic forms in this book:
"Here and there in *Field Work* . . . in 'Casualty', there are
echoes of those short three-stressed lines of middle Yeats"
(Miller, 2000: 39). The consciousness of the craft of poetry
is strong in this book, and in the others which are examined
in this section.

Poetic form becomes of major importance in this period
of his career, as does a diversification of that form. In *Field
Work*, we find lyrics, sonnets of varying degrees of rhythmical
exactitude, translations from Dante, less formal reminis-
cences, formal elegies and a great variation of line length. The
central section of the poem features a sonnet sequence
which brings the contemporary poet very much to the fore
of the book, as the title and dedication illustrate: "Glanmore
Sonnets: for Ann Saddlemyer — our heartiest welcomer".
Here he is writing about himself and his wife in their home;
the mythic world of the first part of *North* is left very much
behind. By availing of the sonnet form, that most literary poetic framework which was transplanted into the English tradition from Renaissance Italy, Heaney is consciously locating his
work within that tradition, though thematically, the sonnets
are firmly located in Ireland, in County Wicklow.

Poetry as a form of communication between self and other is enunciated in the opening line: "Vowels ploughed into other: opened ground" (*FW*, 33). Seeing Glanmore as a "hedge-school" (*FW*, 34), Heaney finds time to write about himself and his rural surroundings. We have already noted his view that it was the similarity between Glanmore and Mossbawn that allowed him to write about the place in which he was living. Here, it is on personal and marital growth that he can concentrate, going on to implicitly compare himself and Marie, his wife, to "Dorothy and William" Wordsworth (*FW*, 35), and to discuss the etymological associations of "boortree" and "elderberry" (*FW*, 37). This poem heralds a preoccupation with language in all its variety, a preoccupation that registers the difference between this and his "first place", Mossbawn (*P*, 18).

Like Wordsworth, his reaction to nature is mediated through language, and indeed, the very fact that Wordsworth and Dorothy are mentioned as a literary couple implies that this response to nature will be literary in tenor and in tone, seeing a cuckoo and corncrake, for example, at twilight as "crepuscular and iambic" (*FW*, 35). Indeed, he places himself and Marie in the context of other literary couples in the final sonnet "Lorenzo and Jessica" and "Diarmuid and Grainne" (*FW*, 42). These couples, one Shakespearian, from *The Merchant of Venice*, and the other Irish, from the *Fiannaíocht* cycle of tales, serve to foreground the literary nature of their rural idyll, though the sequence tends to deconstruct ideas of the rural idyll as it progresses: "as the sequence goes on, the atmosphere darkens" (Vendler, 1998: 67). His hope is that here, in his new home, he will achieve a deeper form of growth: "I will break through . . . what I glazed over" (*FW*, 38). Sonnet VII probes the names of meteorological districts which he heard on the radio in "that strong gale-warning voice" (*FW*, 39), while in the next sonnet, images of violence and fear "Thunderlight on the split logs", "What would I meet, blood-boltered, on the road" cause him to seek sexual comfort: "Come to me quick, I am upstairs and shaking. / My all of you birchwood in lightning" (*FW*, 40). There is a sense that his subjectivity is deepening, and becoming aware of more layers. In Lacan's terms, he is creating a more complex other through which he can engage with aspects of his self.

In the ninth poem of the sequence, Heaney stresses the contradictions that are inherent in his position, contrasting the "burnished bay tree at the gate", a "classical" symbol of honour, with the reality that it is "hung with the reek of silage" from the "next farm". Far from tranquil and idyllic nature, he describes the blood spatters from rats "speared" in the threshing of corn (*FW*, 41) and asks, in this context, two questions which are of central importance to his process of self-questioning: "Did we come to the wilderness for this?" and "What is my apology for poetry?" (*FW*, 41). The other books in this section will attempt to answer both of these questions, as Heaney probes the nature of his art, and the relation of that art to his developing self.

One of the most important aspects of *Field Work* is its focus on the domestic aspect of Heaney's poetry and selfhood. In sonnet X, he recalls their "first night years ago in that hotel", and the experiences which raised them to "the lovely and painful / Covenants of flesh" (*FW*, 42). Heaney made the point that in Glanmore, he and his wife "got married again in a different way" in that they were able to get to know each other more fully: "We started life again together" (Mooney, 1988). Throughout the "Glanmore Sonnets", Marie Heaney is a growing presence, and his use of "we" in this sequence is far more personal and familial than the historical and mythic attitude of the previous two books. His sense of identity is similarly more complex.

"In Memoriam Francis Ledwidge", for example, describes the enigma of a "Tommy's uniform", a "haunted

Catholic face" and traces Ledwidge's own statement of the paradox of being called "a British soldier while my country / Has no place among nations" (*FW*, 60). Ledwidge encompasses the complications of cultural, religious and political identity that are always found by an inquiring mind, and Heaney, whose "field work" in self-identity is carried out through such a process of questioning, makes the point explicit: "In you, our dead enigma, all the strains / Criss-cross in useless equilibrium" (*FW*, 60); useless because Ledwidge is dead and because there was no dynamic interaction in the intersecting strains. This crossing of strains was to become an important theme in both the cultural and political life of Ireland, but in a very useful way.

I would suggest that this poem parallels a growing sense of the complexity of identity in general and of Irish identity in particular. The border was both more permanent and more permeable than one might first imagine. The republican ideal of a united Ireland, itself the stated aim of the largest political party in Ireland, Fianna Fáil, had never really faced the question as to the fate of the unionists, to whom such a notion was anathema. Ironically, the fixity of the unionist position was also coming into question, as Ulster Protestants would partake in, and support, an all-Ireland rugby team, even when playing against England. Ledwidge's position gestures towards the dawnings of such complicated positions, and he seems a possible image of a more tolerant relationship.

This exercise in understanding and tolerance is balanced by the final poem, "Ugolino", a translation from Dante, which enacts the bringing of revenge and hatred from the past into the afterlife, as Count Ugolino spends eternity "gnawing" at the skull of "archbishop Roger", who had starved himself and his family to death. Of course, the image of enemies locked in eternal conflict, avenging the past, is a potent symbol of the Northern conflict. Heaney is all too aware that forces of atavism and essentialism, having been revived, will not disappear too easily. There is still an under-standing of this tribal position, but the book also features an exposure to other responses, and to an ongoing interroga-tion of the very notion of a correct response, a responsible *tristia*. Formally, the use of Dante in this poem, and in "An Afterwards" leads us to the next major collection of this period, *Station Island*, where the imagery of a religious setting and ghostly presences will be further developed, as will the focus on "the music of what happens" (*FW*, 56).

In *Field Work*, his notions of a mythic Irishness, the "we" of "Kinship", who can "slaughter for the common good" are gradually complicated as the "Irishness" which he sees in the Republic of Ireland is far different to the more entrenched positions of the "Irish" (Catholic, nationalist, republican) tra-dition in Northern Ireland: "My people think money / And talk weather" (*FW*, 13). He found a different approach to these issues:

> *North* is a very oblique and intense book. It was fused at a very high pressure, and had to do with all of my past, really, up until that stage. The next poems in *Field Work*, such as "Glanmore Sonnets", are to do with my adult present . . . My adult intelligence was applying itself to the circumstances of my life. (Mur-phy, 2000b: 88)

In *Station Island*, there is an increasing interest in sustained meditations structured around the "circumstances" of Heaney's adult life, so we find in "Shelf Life" a sequence of six poems about particular objects. One of these is a granite chip from "Joyce's Martello Tower", which urges him to "*Seize / the day*" [*italics original*] (*SI*, 21). Here, the poetic process involves investing the quotidian with meaning, as the music of what happens is gradually transformed into a mel-ody with much broader resonances.

The same is true of "Sandstone Keepsake", where a stone, picked from a "shingle beach" on the Inishowen peninsula, reminds him of how, across the bay, lights from the Magilligan internment camp are set off by the motion. He imagines himself watched by "trained binoculars", and being seen as a "silhouette not worth bothering about", someone "not about to set the times wrong or right" (*SI*, 20). His questioning of the role of art in a political situation, of the role of the aesthetic with respect to the political, is being teased out all the time, and the consistent references to Dante underscore this questioning process. Instead, in a manner similar to that of Dante, who was admired by Heaney as being "able to accommodate the political and the transcendent," he wishes to discover a "properly literary activity which might contain a potentially public meaning" (*ER*, 96).

He has gradually discovered that "Glimmerings are what the soul's composed of. / Fogged-up challenges, far conscience-glitters" (*SI*, 23), and it is to these that he must turn, as opposed to the seeming mythic certainties of *North* and the bog poems. Just as his sojourn at Glanmore placed poetry at the centre of his life, so now his poetic focus is more on poetry itself, and on literature about poetry. His title "Making Strange" would immediately resonate with any student of literary theory as recalling the Russian formalist idea that all art consisted in defamiliarising objects from their usual context in order to see them anew. He seems to be coming to the conclusion that part of the function of art is to attempt to see things in a new light:

> reciting my pride
> in all that I knew, that began to make strange
> at that same recitation. (*SI*, 33)

Thus, in "The Birthplace", he is able to make a liberating comment on place, that concept which was so central to the earlier books, where it was shot through with connotations of racial and communal identity and territoriality. Now, speaking of the birthplace of another writer, Thomas Hardy, he can say:

> Everywhere being nowhere,
> Who can prove
> one place more than another? (*SI*, 35)

This is emblematic of the process at work in this section of Heaney's work, as he takes cultural, linguistic and historical givens, and attempts to transcend them through his writing. Whereas in *North*, he used his art to utter the concerns of his tribe, in this section, he will attempt to transform that consciousness through a focus on his own growth. This will be the driving force behind the central sequence of this book, the poems that comprise "Station Island" itself.

Saint Patrick's Purgatory is an island in Lough Derg in County Donegal, which has been a site of Roman Catholic pilgrimage since medieval times. Given what I have identified as Heaney's developmental project of moving away from group identities and towards a more individual sense of self-hood, we might well join Catherine Byron in asking why Heaney sets an act of "poetic autobiography" in a site of a "devotional exercise at the heart of the unregenerate patriarchy of Irish Catholicism?" (Byron, 1992: 18). Perhaps the Dantean presence would give some clue, as Heaney's pilgrimage has some measure of parallel with the *Divine Comedy* of Dante in that Heaney will explore a spectral underworld, where spirits will visit him, as opposed to Dante's poem where he and Virgil visited the souls of the dead. As he put it: "all I needed was a journey, a place that would be both a realistic setting and a congregating area for all kinds of shades" (Miller, 2000: 34).

Heaney has made the point, in "Envies and Identifications: Dante and the Modern Poet", that Dante's *Purgatorio* has been an immense influence on his work, specifically in terms of the nature of the relationship between poetry and politics. What Dante demonstrated to Heaney was the way "Dante could place himself in an historical world yet submit that world to scrutiny from a perspective beyond history, the way he could accommodate the political and the transcendent" (*EI*, 18). The mode of pilgrimage allowed Dante to use the journey metaphor to catalogue changes and developments in himself. For Heaney, this would prove to be a potent symbolic avenue through which he could explore the "typical strains which the consciousness labours under in this country . . . to be faithful to the collective historical experience and to be true to the recognitions of the emerging self" (*EI*, 18–19). In formal terms, Heaney has made the point about section VII that he liked the "muted rhyming, the slightly Dantesque formality of the verse" (Miller, 2001: 25). As Dominic Manganiello has put it: "When modern poets turn to the great masters of the past, they do so in order to fill their own imaginative needs" (Manganiello, 2000, 101).

He is thus able to create the ghosts to act as mirror images or refractions of aspects of his own personality. His first ghost, Simon Sweeney, exemplifies this qualified assent to the demands of pilgrimage. He is "an old Sabbath-breaker" (*SI*, 61), who adjures Heaney to "stay clear of all processions" (*SI*, 63). The second ghost was William Carleton, who had written *The Lough Derg Pilgrim* in 1828. He had converted to Protestantism, and this book was intended to serve "as a piece of anti-Papist propaganda" (Parker, 1993: 183). Heaney, in section I, has Carleton call himself a "traitor", and give the advice that "it is a road you travel on your own" (*SI*, 65), terms which illustrate the guilt associated with leaving a communal religious identity. Carleton's advice to the poet is to "remember everything and keep your head"

(*SI*, 66). Patrick Kavanagh, a poet who had exerted a strong early influence on Heaney, and who also wrote about Lough Derg, appears in Section V. His comment is similarly scathing: "Forty-two years on / and you've got no farther!" (*SI*, 73), and all three figures voice Heaney's frustration that parts of his psyche have not yet outgrown the societal and religious givens of his culture.

Another meeting is with the shade of a "young priest, glossy as a blackbird". This was Terry Keenen, whom Heaney knew as a clerical student (Corcoran, 1998: 117). However, the priest describes his time in the missions, an experience that was far from enabling: "Everything wasted. / I rotted like a pear. I sweated masses" (*SI*, 69). It is a vision of the priest which Heaney had never imagined, seeing him as "some sort of holy mascot" who "gave too much relief" and "raised a siege" among those whom he visited: "doing the decent thing" (*SI*, 70). However, the response of the shade is sharp and in keeping with those of Carleton and Kavanagh: "What are you doing, going through these motions?", he asks, and goes on to supply a possible answer: "Unless you are here taking the last look" (*SI*, 71).

Both Carleton and Kavanagh stress the need for change: "O holy Jesus Christ, does nothing change?", cries Carleton on being told that Heaney is setting out to "do the station" (*SI*, 64), while the shade of Kavanagh sarcastically comments that he "might have known" that, having "made the pad" Heaney would follow him "sooner or later" (*SI*, 73). The young priest, on being seen by Heaney as "doomed to the decent thing", responds in kind:

> I at least was young and unaware
>
> That what I thought was chosen was convention.
> But all this you were clear of you walked into

Over again. And the god has, as they say, withdrawn."
(*SI*, 70)

Here, Heaney asks himself, through the persona of the priest, the difficult question of why he is still in search of this group identification. He is able to see the flaws in the role of the priest, "doomed to do the decent thing", but is repeating such a path himself. It is yet another imaging of the difficulty involved in outgrowing the conventions and ideological positions that are part of our inheritance.

Perhaps the most important aspect of this sequence is that it allows Heaney to speak through the personalities of others. Through these encounters with different ghosts, he is able to give voice to doubts and uncertainties, using these personalities as sounding boards to enunciate different perspectives. Behind all of these voices is the developing voice of Heaney himself, furthering the process of questioning that we saw initiated in "Exposure" and developed through the elegies in *Field Work*, particularly in the person of Louis O'Neill in "Casualty". These different figures allow him to question aspects of unconscious filiation to the religious, the cultural and the domestic that have lain dormant and unquestioned until this point in his adult life. In a very real way, this pilgrimage is to the island of the unconscious within his own mind: he is in search of himself as opposed to anything else, and specifically in search of the answerability between his art and his culture.

In terms of the political entanglements that have been part of his heritage, "Station Island" also provides opportunities for questions. Sidney Burris sees these poems as based on an investigation of the relationship between the "artistic imperative and the political conscience" (Burris, 1990: 146), and while this is true, I would argue that what is actually at stake here is a process of redefinition of this relationship. In section VII, he mentions William Strathearn who was killed

by being "called down to the shop door in the middle of the
night" and shot (Miller, 2001: 25). Strathearn tells the story
of his death, of being awoken, called downstairs to open the
shop to get "pills / or a powder or something in a bottle"
for two men: "I knew them both" (*SI*, 78). Telling the story,
he makes much of the fact that the men were "barefaced as
they would be in the day, // shites thinking they were the be-
all and the end-all" (*SI*, 79). The matter-of-fact tone highlights the finality of death, a death of one of the victims who
were so easily consigned to historical processes in "Kinship". Heaney asks this shade to "Forgive the way I have
lived, indifferent — / forgive my timid, circumspect involvement" (*SI*, 80). Here we see the pull of the political appetites
of gravity, as Heaney feels that as a nationalist with a public
profile, as "Seamus Heaney", the name in inverted commas,
he could have done more to voice his own people's cause.

This accusation is made directly in Section VIII by the
shade of Colum McCartney, Heaney's cousin and the subject
of "The Strand at Lough Beg" in *Field Work*. He reminds
Heaney that he was "with poets when you got the word",
and stayed with them while his "own flesh and blood" was
brought to Bellaghy (*SI*, 82). He goes on to accuse Heaney of
having "whitewashed ugliness", adding that:

> You confused evasion with artistic tact
> The Protestant who shot me through the head
> I accuse directly, but indirectly, you. (*SI*, 83)

The third voice from the political world is that of hunger
striker Francis Hughes, and the poem (section IX) opens
with a gesture towards the bog imagery of the earlier books:
"My brain dried like spread turf', as the IRA man recalls his
career: "a hit-man on the brink, emptied and deadly" (*SI*, 84).
Here is the voice of militant nationalism: the response to the
killings of Colum McCartney and William Strathearn, and
there is an aspect of Heaney that feels that he should have,

at times, adopted a more militant stance: "I hate how quick I was to know my place." (*SI*, 85).

What this interplay of the religious, literary and sexual voices from his past achieves is a dawning of perspective, a realisation that his reaction to his culture and to the historical situation of that culture must be individual: he is not, nor can he be, the saviour of his tribe. The notion, expressed in *North*, of luring "the tribal shoals to epigram / And order", and the feelings of guilt at his inability to create a salvific art have now been replaced with a more realistic assessment of the role of the individual. As he puts it at the end of the section: "As if the cairnstone could defy the cairn. / As if the eddy could reform the pool." (*SI*, 86).

This prefigures the advice given by the Joycean shade in the final section of the poem. Focusing on a temporal coincidence, that "Stephen's Diary / for April the thirteenth", what he calls "the Feast of the Holy Tundish" is the same date as Heaney's own birthday, he rehearses Joyce's discussion of notions of belonging and identity in *A Portrait of the Artist as a Young Man*. Here, Stephen, in a conversation with the English dean of studies, refers to a tundish, an instrument which the dean calls a funnel. This causes Stephen to ponder the colonial heritage of the English language in Ireland: "The language in which we are speaking is his before it is mine. How different are the words *home, Christ, ale, master*, on his lips and on mine!" (Joyce, 1993: 166). However, in the actual entry for 13 April, the perspective is altered — "That tundish has been on my mind for a long time. I looked it up and find it is English and good old blunt English too" (Joyce, 1993: 217) — as Joyce complicates the postcolonial issues involved.

In "Station Island", Joyce is similarly dismissive of Heaney's "peasant pilgrimage", urging him to focus on his own personal growth, as opposed to that "subject people stuff" which he calls "a cod's game" (*SI*, 93). In the closing

poem of the "Station Island" sequence (to which he is referring in the above quotation), he has Joyce encourage this
process of refutation:

> Your obligation
> is not discharged by any common rite.
> What you must do must be done on your own
>
> so get back in harness. The main thing is to write
> for the joy of it. Cultivate a work-lust. (*SI*, 92–3)

In his advice to Heaney (and it is well to remember that the
actual speaker here is Heaney himself), Joyce carries on in
the same vein, urging Heaney to "Take off from here" and to
"Let go, let fly, forget." He goes on to stress the importance
of taking control of his own future as opposed to remaining
passive in terms of the past: "You've listened long enough.
Now strike your note" (*SI*, 93). The similarity with the earlier advice of McLaverty in "Fosterage" — "Listen. Go your
own way. / Do your own work" (*N*, 71) — is clear, connecting the end of *North* with this section of *Station Island*.

   In ways, this is a continuation of the debate that was explored in "Exposure", where Heaney wondered about his
audience; or in "Glanmore Sonnets" where he wondered
about his "apology for poetry". Now, in terms of the relationship between the individual and his community, he has
come to a decisive point: the Ireland of the mind to which
he will turn will be an imaginative one, predicated on present and future, and will be written about on his own terms:

> Keep at a tangent.
> When they make the circle wide, it's time to swim
>
> out on your own and fill the element
> with signatures on your own frequency. (*SI*, 93–4)

Perhaps the most important legacy of "Station Island" is the redefinition of place, a redefinition that we first saw advanced in "The Birthplace", as empty of all predestined presence, as somewhere that, far from enforcing its history on an individual, would instead take the shape of that individual's ideas and perceptions of place. As he puts it:

> I thought of walking round
> and round a space utterly empty,
> utterly a source, like the idea of sound. (*HL*, 68)

That a source is an idea is central to his process of questioning the relationship between the individual and the group. His reconceptualising of *place* in order to create a *space*: "allows for an exploration of the difference within sameness that is central to all ethical discourse" (O'Brien, 1999a: 8), and facilitates his deconstruction of the givens of identity. Having analysed this inclination in his first four books (place), he uses these four to analyse his own attempts to develop as an individual (space). This mode of thinking places Heaney in the intellectual ambit of poststructuralist and postmodernist theories of source and origin. Derrida, in particular, with his deconstruction of simplified notions of presence, of an authority that is beyond the movement or play of any system of thought, would provide parallel here. From delving into the psychic memory of his community's sense of historical grievance in *North*, and from attempting to speak out of that psychic centre, Heaney now is looking for plural sources of selfhood, and for a more fluid and distanced relationship with place.

Perhaps one aspect of this space is that it stands for facets of Heaney's self, which are in the process of becoming, as opposed to merely taking on the colours of their culture and history. His relationship with place has been transformed, from an artesian probing of the psychic communal

memory bank to a more individualistic translating and transforming of that past into a personalised aesthetic wherein
the relationship with tradition is more nuanced and the perspective is more transcendental than immanent. The
Sweeney figure symbolises this distancing effect, as his relationship with his native place is one of exile and transformation: he is also an inner émigré, albeit of a different order of
being. He was the king of Dal-Aire in mid-Ulster, who was
cursed by Saint Ronan and turned into a bird who was forced
to fly all over Ireland. Heaney's preoccupation with the
Sweeney figure can be understood in terms of this altered
relationship with place, both in terms of his phonetic similarity with Heaney's own name, and also his tortured relationship with place and history. As Deane puts it, "immediately
after the Joycean encounter that closes the central sequence
in *Station Island*, Heaney takes his own advice and becomes
Sweeney" (Deane, 1996: 31).

In his introduction to *Sweeney Astray*, Heaney writes of
the poem in a manner which is deeply connected to the mo-
tivating concerns of the "Station Island" sequence, as he
notes that:

> Insofar as Sweeney is also a figure of the artist, dis-
> placed, guilty, assuaging himself by his utterance, it is
> possible to read the work as an aspect of the quarrel
> between free creative imagination and the con-
> straints of religious, political and domestic obligation.
> (*SA*, viii)

That these concerns parallel the concerns of the Dante-
inspired "Station Island" sequence is clear, as Sweeney is
doubly incarnated in Heaney's work, figuring in the final section of *Station Island*, and in a full translation of the tale, entitled *Sweeney Astray*. For Heaney, the figure of a king, transformed into a bird and forced to fly all over Ireland — "He
shall roam Ireland, mad and bare" (*SA*, 15) — has a poetic

and politic significance, as it demonstrates a different, more distanced, relationship between person and place. Sweeney is in internal exile: "God has exiled me from myself" (*SA*, 19). The appearance of Sweeney in both the translation and in the final part of *Station Island* demonstrates the fluidity of the symbol for Heaney. He is a symbol of a new type of imagined Ireland, and of a different, dislocated relationship with place and tradition. As Heaney puts it in the notes at the end of the book:

> A version of the Irish tale is available in my *Sweeney Astray*, but I trust these glosses can survive without the support system of the original story. Many of them, of course, are imagined in contexts far removed from early medieval Ireland. (*SI*, 123)

The point here is that Sweeney becomes a symbol of the artist, a paradigm of the Joycean figure of Stephen Dedalus and his prototype, the Greek Daedalus, who attempted to transcend the maze in Crete. In a sense, Heaney/Sweeney will attempt to transcend the difficulties of his own cultural maze through a similar poetic transformation.

The original story concerns Sweeney, the king of "Dal-Aire" who was angered by Saint Ronan's making of a church in his lands. He discovered the saint, reading from his "psalter" (an illuminated book) and in a fit of anger "flung it into the cold depths of a lake nearby" (*SA*, 14), and is cursed by Ronan. Later, before the battle of Moira, all the armies are sprinkled with holy water, and Sweeney, thinking this has been done to mock him, threw a spear and "killed one of Ronan's psalmists in a single cast". A second spear pierced the "bell that hung" from Ronan's neck (*SA*, 16). Ronan curses Sweeney "to the trees, / bird-brain among branches" (*SA*, 17). The metamorphosis of Sweeney from man to bird is described in violent terms, with the lurching rhythms of the language enacting the change in form of Sweeney:

> His brain convulsed,
> His mind split open.
> Vertigo, hysteria, lurchings
> And launchings came over him . . .
> and he levitated in a frantic cumbersome motion
> like a bird in the air. (*SA*, 18)

The physical effort, pain and difficulty of such a change is captured both in the language and in the dislocated rhythm of the description. Forced to take to the air, the rest of the poem mingles laments on the part of Sweeney with some beautiful descriptions of the places which he visits.

The sound system of this poem is worthy of comment as the sound of Christianity, the monotone of "the clink of Ronan's bell" (*SA*, 13) is contrasted with the sounds that Sweeney hears in his travels around Ireland: "the Bann cuckoo, calling sweeter / than church bells that whinge and grind" (*SA*, 25); "Bolcain, that happy glen of winds / and wind-borne echoes" (*SA*, 29); "this bleating / and belling in the glen . . . startles my heartstrings" (*SA*, 39). This theme reaches its climax as he says that:

> I prefer the elusive
> rhapsody of blackbirds
> to the garrulous blather
> of men and women. (*SA*, 44)

However, to see this poem as a *paean* of praise to such transformations would be to misread it, as Sweeney constantly laments what he has lost. I would suggest that it is in the dialectic between praise of his new Ireland, and lamentation over that which he has lost, that the meaning of this poem is to be found.

Sweeney regrets his loss of kingdom and humanity, as he puts it: "I am haggard, womanless, / and cut off from music" (*SA*, 19). From the beginning, the physical difficulty of his newly acquired skills of flight is foregrounded, as the following list of verbs of motion clearly indicates: "poking"; "shouldering"; "unsettling"; "wading"; "breasting"; "trekking" . . . while the physical difficulty of this new environment is similarly set out: "thorny twigs would flail him" so that he was "prickled and cut and bleeding all over". He lives among "thick briars" on a "thorny bed" and looks like a "man in a bloodbath" by the time he is finished (*SA*, 21). There are passages of lyric lament, beginning with the word "no" throughout the book: "no sleep, no respite, / no hope for a long time" (*SA*, 22), and his sense of loss is keenly felt throughout. On hearing of his son's death, he voices the following beautiful lament:

> Ah! Now the gallows trap has opened
> That drops the strongest to the ground!
> A haunted father's memory
> Of his small boy calling *Daddy*!
>
> This is a blow I cannot stand. (*SA*, 36)

Immediately on hearing this news, Sweeney "fell from the yew tree" (*SA*, 37), demonstrating that while utterance can assuage the self, it can neither undo nor ameliorate events that occur.

When he is on Ailsa Craig, off the coast of Scotland, a "bell-shaped rock" symbolising a connection with Ronan's bell, the source of his exile, Sweeney is at a low ebb. He sees it as "a hard station" (a phrase harking back to *Station Island*) which causes his nails to be "bent", his "loins weak", his "feet bleeding" and his "thighs bare" (*SA*, 52). His only recourse is his imagination:

> And imagine treelines
> Somewhere beyond,
> A banked-up, soothing,
> Wooded haze. (*SA*, 52–3)

Importantly, it does not ameliorate his situation, nor offer any long-term solutions. Like Heaney, Sweeney's art is all that he can offer, with little hope of any external effect. His imagination allows him some measure of comfort by voicing his hope and despair, as well as by creating an imaginative inner world which makes his acceptance of the outer world easier. Through the creation of an imagined place, the realities of the actual place can be, to a degree at least, transcended. Perhaps the most interesting effect of Sweeney's internal exile is an altered perspective on his part as to the rights of others. His exile has resulted from an intolerance of another encroaching on his territory, an intolerance of a different tradition.

As Heaney put it in his introduction, Sweeney is a "literary creation" and not a "given figure of myth or legend"; but he goes on:

> the literary imagination which fastened upon him as an image was clearly in the grip of a tension between the newly dominant Christian ethos and the older, recalcitrant Celtic temperament. (*SA*, vii)

He explains that it is equally important:

> to dwell upon Sweeney's easy sense of cultural affinity with both western Scotland and southern Ireland as exemplary for all men and women in contemporary Ulster, or to ponder the thought that this Irish invention may well have been a development of a British original, vestigially present in the tale of the madman called Alan. (*SA*, viii)

Here, the ability to inhabit both cultures, each a source of the two contending traditions in Northern Ireland, allows for a different level of meaning within the poem's reception.

In terms of the new incarnations of Sweeney that we see in "Sweeney Redivivus" from *Station Island*, he is an image of Heaney's "book of changes" (*SI*, 121), as he becomes a paradigm of the discovery of that "properly literary activity which might contain a potentially public meaning" (*ER*, 96). We are reminded of the poem "Changes" earlier in the book, where the idea of a "bird's eye view" was first mooted. In the opening poem of this section "The First Gloss", he talks about the "first step taken" into "the margin" (*SI*, 97), and this step would be following the advice of the Joycean *persona* at the end of the "Station Island" sequence. In the next two poems, the metaphor of a "ball of wet twine" (*SI*, 98) which is gradually unwinding becomes symbolic of Heaney's own unwinding of the tight ball of guilt and sense of attachment to his own tradition, which we saw so clearly in *North*. Sweeney becomes an image now of an imagined Heaney "there I was, incredible to myself" (*SI*, 98). He explains this sense of artistic freedom in "Unwinding":

> So the twine unwinds and loosely widens
> backward through areas that forwarded
> understandings of all I would undertake. (*SI*, 99)

The complex interaction of past, present, future and future conditional, as embodied in the different tenses in this short stanza, is rendered more achievable through the persona of Sweeney. His transformation is a paradigm of what Heaney is attempting to bring about in his poetry; it is the result of that process of questioning that we noted in "Exposure", in *North*, and in "Casualty" in *Field Work*. At the close of *Station Island*, Heaney speaks of the "spirit" breaking cover to "raise a dust / in the font of exhaustion" (*SI*, 121). As Stan Smith perceptively notes, as well as signifying a holy water font (Corcoran, 1998: 133), this is also "the font of print itself, which is where all new texts find their origins" (Smith, 1992: 60). It is also where the "book of changes" finds its origin, and the act of imaginative writing is the release valve through which the "long dumbfounded" spirit finds its voice. There is nothing simple in terms of the correct or responsible reaction to the complexities of history (a point that will be further explored in *An Open Letter*), and the unwinding of the filiations of tradition, paralleling those of family that we saw in "Digging", is an important step in this process.

For example, the givens of history, the rights and wrongs, when viewed from this "unwound" perspective, take on different colourings: "The royal roads were cow paths. / The queen mother hunkered on a stool" (*SI*, 101). Here we have, in microcosm, an image of the revisionist trend in historiography that was a result of the Northern Irish violence. Historians began to unpack the hagiographic structure through which the events from 1916 to 1922 had been viewed, and the result was a more layered perspective on the originary events of the Republic of Ireland. The desire for a consistent form of response, having been deconstructed by the different personae of the "Station Island" sequence, is further deconstructed here, as he is, through the voice of Sweeney, able to admit: "I blew hot and blew cold" (*SI*, 101).

This is stated explicitly in "The First Flight" where the Sweeney persona is credited with transforming Heaney's perspective: "I was mired in attachment" (*SI*, 102), he says "so I mastered new rungs of the air / to survey out of reach / their bonfires on hills" (*SI*, 103). Through Sweeney, he has been able to take the advice of Joyce, and of Simon Sweeney: "Stay clear of all processions!" (*SI*, 63), and to gradually discover that the role of the artist is to "rent / the veil of the usual" (*SI*, 104). As he puts it, the identification he

made "between the green man and the rural child was ad-
mitted and even stimulated. Sweeney was unreservedly
rhymed with Heaney" (*ER*, 100), and he goes on to quote
the concluding stanza of "The Cleric":

> Give him his due, in the end
> he opened my path to a kingdom
> of such scope and neuter allegiance
> my emptiness reigns at its whim. (*SI*, 108)

Clearly, there is a personal and contemporary dimension to
the association of Heaney with Sweeney. Sweeney is one of
the poetic devices, signified by the felicitous rhyme with
Heaney's own name, which allows him to find his "door into
the light" and which allows him to use "I" to refer to himself: "Now I live by a famous strand" (*SI*, 118), referring to
his home in Dublin, which is close to Sandymount Strand.
Through this persona, and those of the "Station Island" sequence, he is able to put history in the past, as explained in
"The Old Icons" where he talks of a "patriot with folded
arms" and "the outlawed priest's / red vestments". Even
though he has been able to do this, he still feels some measure of attachment: "Why, when it was all over, did I hold on
to them?" (*SI*, 117). He is still able to understand these attachments, though he is now also becoming able to contex-
tualise them as part of his own persona, as opposed to the
whole.

The Sweeney connection has helped to bring this about,
as he puts it in "Earning a Rhyme":

> I began to inflate myself and my situation into
> Sweeney's, to make analogies between the early me-
> dieval Ulsterman who rocketed out of the north, as
> a result of vehement squabble there among the petty
> dynasties, and this poet from Co. Derry who had

>   also come south for purposes of retreat and compo-
>   sure. (*ER*, 98)

Here, the connections between Heaney and Sweeney become overt, as in terms of the poem, Heaney carries on his
programme of questioning the socio-cultural givens of the
Northern Irish situation by looking at the nature of the conflict and the name "Ulster". He notes that the term originally
named an Irish province and formed part of a "native Gaelic
cosmology", but has become, through plantation in the
1620s and partition in the 1920s "the name of a six-county
British enclave that resisted integration with the Republic of
Ireland" (*ER*, 96–7). This probing of names and identities has
become part of Heaney's ongoing interrogation of his cultural heritage, and he makes the point that he hoped this
poem would "not threaten a unionist" while at the same
time it might fortify a nationalist by making a unionist audience aware of "the notion that Ulster was Irish, without co-
ercing them out of their cherished conviction that it was
British" (*ER*, 97). He is not looking for a victory in his writing: he is looking for forms of negotiation between traditions.

We see this idea more overtly expressed in *An Open Letter*, the *Field Day* pamphlet wherein Heaney takes issue with
his inclusion in *The Penguin Book of Contemporary British Poetry*, edited by Blake Morrison and Andrew Motion. Here,
on first reading, he would appear to be voicing a nationalist
objection to being called "British"; this looks like a classic
post-colonial rejection of a literary colonialism, thus placing
Heaney firmly within the mindset of the Irish nationalist, republican tradition. As he puts it, "My anxious muse . . . Has
to refuse // The adjective" (*OL*, 7), and he goes on to high-
light the opposition between "*Britannia*" a "united England,
Scotland, Wales" and "*Hibernia*" [*italics original*] where:

> . . . the Gaels
> Made a last stand
>
> And long ago were stood upon —
> End of simple history lesson. (*OL*, 7)

Here, in the final clause, that ongoing process of decon-structing what seems to be a simple assertion that we have traced through all of his work is again apparent. The rest of the pamphlet, following on the end of the "simple history lesson" proceeds to complicate the context of that history, to the extent that any simplistic reading of this pamphlet as Heaney voicing an anti-British sentiment is rendered incor-rect.

His teasing out of the intricacies of the relationship be-tween *Hibernia* and *Britannia*, and of his own position within this relationship has similarities with his discussion of the complexity of the term "Ulster" in "Earning a Rhyme", and with the different attitudes to history in "Sweeney Redivi-vus". He traces the complexity of his position with clarity. He has been called a "British" poet before and "acquiesced" (*OL*, 7). For "weeks and months" he has "messed about / Unclear, embarrassed and in doubt" as to whether to "write it out / Or let it go" (*OL*, 8). Indeed, he readily admits that there are good reasons for classifying him as a British poet: he publishes in "LRB and TLS, / *The Listener*"; his audience is "Via Faber // a British one" (*OL*, 9). He is willing to see that, like the notion of "Ulster" of which he spoke in "Earning a Rhyme", the ideas of being Irishness or Britishness are com-plicated, as they are imagined constructs.

As Molino puts it, Heaney is aware that he is as much a product of the British literary tradition as he is of the Irish one (Molino, 1994: 120). However, while this is accurate up to a point, it does not present the full picture of what is at work in this poem. We must recall the phrase "end of sim-

ple history lesson", as it provides an important answer to
some of Heaney's ongoing questions. It is not so much a
question of the Irish–British binarism that is at work here;
rather, is it a new "commonwealth of art" (*OL*, 9) which sub-
sumes both sets of identities into a different order. This is
one of the earliest manifestations of his architectonic urge to
create structures which will be sufficiently complex to include all aspects of identity. From the beginning of this most
allusive of poems, Heaney has been blending names and quo-
tations for the Irish and British literary traditions with those
of other cultures to create this very commonwealth within
the letter — an "open" letter, open to new influences.

The final quotation, from the work of Miroslav Holub,
discusses the Aesopic fable of a man yelling out in a cinema
when "a beaver's called a muskrat / By the narrator" of a
film (*OL*, 12). This point is the kernel of the poem:

> Names were not for negotiation.
> Right names were the first foundation
>   For telling truth. (*OL*, 13)

The audience of this film are unimpressed by his outburst
and want him to be thrown out. However, for Heaney, it is
this issue of "right names" and a notion of personal "truth"
that is of prime importance. Having set out to use the "I" to
mean himself in his contemporary, adult life, he now voices
the need for truth in terms of the complications of the identity of that "I". No longer "mired in attachment", nevertheless, he has created an Ireland of the mind in these books,
and it is to this notion of Ireland that he is loyal in this open
letter. He will go on to develop this vision of Ireland in the
next books.

Chapter Three

A Pure Change Happened

The Irelands of the mind created by Heaney in his work have been radically different, and the same can be said of his next series of books. In this chapter, we will examine *The Haw Lantern* and *Seeing Things* and show how these collections further complicate his notions of Ireland and Irishness. He develops the notion of space as a source, validating absence as well as presence, in terms of language and the subjective "I", a process that has echoes of Lacan's idea of the subject as always striving for a wholeness which will always escape it. Necessarily, issues of identity will always be open to question and any sense of presence or fullness, while desirable, will always prove to be elusive. Thus, Ireland will invariably disperse into different Irelands, and the same is true of Irishness itself. The focus now will be less on a sense of communal identity — the "we" — and instead, more on the individual — the "I".

There is a surety of purpose and a strong sense of self-confidence to be found in the lyric "I" of all of these books, and it is best captured by two epigraphs in *The Haw Lantern*. The epigraph to the book itself demonstrates the transforming power of language: "The riverbed, dried-up, half-full of leaves. / Us, listening to a river in the trees" (*HL*, vii). This image is more complex than it seems on first reading: does

he mean the sound of wind in the trees is like a river, or
does he mean that the rustling of the leaves in the riverbed
is like a river in the trees, or does he mean both at the same
time? In a book where presence and absence interact in a
dialectical fashion, this epigraph sets the tone, as it develops
the ghostly images of the "Station Island" sequence, as well
as the presence–absence oscillation in the Heaney–Sweeney
relationship.

The second epigraph is to the sonnet sequence "Clearances", written in dedication to his mother, who had re-
cently died. Referring to a lesson which his mother had
taught him, about the ability to split "the biggest block of
coal" by getting the "grain and hammer angled right", he
goes on:

> The sound of that relaxed alluring blow,
> Its co-opted and obliterated echo . . .
> Taught me between the hammer and the block
> To face the music. (HL, 24) [*italics original*]

This image of sound, echo and obliteration of the echo symbolises an attitude of confidence which is used to face up to
difficult issues which he has hitherto tried to avoid. His earlier doubts about the value of writing in the face of a political
crisis have been worked through. In the opening poem of *The
Haw Lantern*, "Alphabets", he is able to discuss the steps from
reality to writing, as he traces how, initially, the letters of the
alphabet were recognised through their similarity to shapes
with which his childhood self would have been familiar.
Speaking of himself in the third person, thereby achieving
some of the aesthetic distance which the ghosts and Sweeney
persona achieved in *Station Island*, he tells of how his initial
contact with images was a "shadow his father makes with
joined hands". He goes on to describe his initial contact with
letter and number through familiar metaphors: "the forked
stick that they call Y" and the swan's neck and back that

"Make the 2", while "Two rafters and a cross-tie on the slate" represent the letter "some call *ah*, some call *ay*", and a globe "in the window tilts like a coloured O" (*HL*, 1).

In this poem about signs, he traces his development through different levels of writing and language. He moves on to the different names for the activity, first "copying out" and then "English", but he is still in the realm of connecting this activity with the physical givens of his early environment, as his work is marked "correct with a little leaning hoe" (*HL*, 1). His development through "Book One of *Elementa Latina*" is charted, and interestingly, in this and subsequent books, there is an ongoing classical frame of reference to be found, as Heaney's imagined Ireland is voiced through his interaction with different aspects of the European classical literary tradition. In "Alphabets" he explains how he "left the Latin forum" for a new "calligraphy which felt like home", and again, the letters are compared to the natural world: "The capitals were orchards in full bloom / The lines of script like briars coiled in ditches" (*HL*, 2). Again, the world of language and sign is seen in terms of the physical world. While describing a gradual growth in learning, the world of imagination is still governed by the physical experience of the speaker of the poem. What we see in this poem is that progression from the referent, the thing in the world, to the sign, the linguistic or poetic symbol of that physicality:

> Balers drop bales like printouts where stooked sheaves
> Made lambdas on the stubble once at harvest
> And the delta face of each potato pit
> Was patted straight. (*HL*, 2–3)

Here, language is mediating his vision of reality: the sign, or signifier, has become dominant over the referent. This is a poem aware of semiotics, and of Saussurean theories of language as mediating reality. His education in language and symbol has allowed him to internalise the linguistic processes so that they become mediating factors in his interaction with the world: language no longer reflects reality, it now can shape it.

This is enacted by the three O's in the poem. The first is the globe in the window of his school, which is compared, in simile, to a "coloured O", making it the first example of the sign being used as a comparative for an object, itself a simulacrum; up to this, the process was reversed. In the third section of the poem we are told the "globe has spun". He stands in a "wooden O", the "Shakespearian 'wooden O' of a lecture theatre" (Corcoran, 1998: 142), lecturing on "English" and on poetry: he has moved from student to teacher, from reader to writer, from passive acceptance to creation of his world through language. His worldview is now mediated by language as opposed to shaping his reaction to language. Now, instead of seeing letters in terms of their similarities to forked sticks or swans or cross-ties on slates, he sees natural phenomena in terms of letters. The image of the globe spinning is that of the power of language to enact and inform change and transformation, a process that is completed in the final "O", which again refers to a globe and a window:

> As from his small window
> The astronaut sees all he has sprung from,
> The risen, aqueous, singular, lucent O
> Like a magnified or buoyant ovum. (*HL*, 3)

Here, his beginning has become his end as the spaceship symbolises the completely transformative perspective that is brought about by language, sign and symbol.

Vendler refers to this book as one of "second thoughts" (Vendler, 1998: 122), and this phrase comes from "Terminus", where he discusses the complexity of his own position within his tradition: "Baronies, parishes met where I was born" and the juxtaposition of the British political term "baronies" with that of the Irish Catholic "parish" makes the point economically, as does the idea of carrying two buckets at the same time: "I grew up in between" (*HL*, 5). Here, the notion of the "I" that we saw being unfolded or unwound in the last books is further developed as different aspects of his individuality are afforded "second thoughts" in a series of broadly political poems, four of them connected by anaphoric titles: "From the Frontier of Writing", "From the Republic of Conscience", "From the Land of the Unspoken" and "From the Canton of Expectation", with two more, "The Mud Vision" and "Parable Island" completing the sequence.

In all of these poems, the reader is unsure as to whether Heaney is writing from within these places, or whether he has just come from them. This deliberate level of ambiguity is part of the ethical strength of these poems, as he attempts to write in a broadly political way without returning to the obliquities of *North*. This new departure has not found universal acclaim, with Terence Brown seeing the poems as "collapsing into banality" (Brown, 1992: 190). They are a new departure, evidencing Heaney's increasing interest in poets from Eastern Europe who tend to write, for obvious political reasons, in this gnomic and parabolic style. Michael Allen sees these poems as providing "a vantage point and a new mask" for Heaney (Allen, 1992: 204).

Thus, in "Parable Island", a poem about language, tradition and the different beliefs of a country, he might be referring to Northern Ireland "an occupied nation" whose "only border is an inland one" (*HL*, 10), or then again, he might not, as there are no referential connections to make this certain. Thus Heaney is able to speak about Ireland, and yet avoid doing so at the same time. I would suggest that this is a logical development of the presence/absence trope that has been an increasingly important factor of his poetic development. He can now examine the importance of language and naming, a topic explored in the land and language poems of *Wintering Out*, but from a more distanced perspective. So the "mountain of the shifting names" called, variously "Cape Basalt", the "Sun's Headstone" and the "Orphan's Tit" may parallel the shifting names of "Ulster", "Northern Ireland", the "North", the "Province", or again, it may not. The difference between this pragmatic plurality of names, and the optative desire that "(some day)" the "ore of truth" will be mined from a place underneath this mountain where "all the names converge" (*HL*, 10), is the difference between the early and the late Heaney.

In a different context, this is a restatement, or a second thought, of the immanent position he had adopted in *North*, and the bog poems, but from a different perspective. The pronouns here are interesting: "he" is used, as is a colloquial "you". The voice of the poem has achieved a Sweeney-like perspective in that it hovers above the concerns of the "forked-tongued natives". Hence, he is able to discuss the religious strand of nationalist ideology from this external perspective, using an ironic tone to describe the "one-eyed all-creator" (*HL*, 10). This deity, presiding over an "autochthonous tradition" (*HL*, 11), is reminiscent of the monocular citizen in Joyce's *Ulysses*, and has a single vision of identity and belonging, as well as being a male incarnation of the "goddess" of the earlier poems. In this "second thought", what interests Heaney more than anything is the way in which narratives of identity are created and read.

Hence, while the "missionary scribes" recall an "autochthonous tradition" celebrated by the single note of the "one bell-tower", Heaney observes that: "you can't be sure that parable is not / at work already retrospectively" (*HL*, 10–11), making the point that in narrative, be it historical or otherwise, there is always an agenda at work in the telling. Here, he is close to the postmodern idea that stories shape our lives, and that language and narrative are ideologically charged. As he puts it in the poem, some saw the "stone circles" as "pure symbol" while others saw them as "assembly spots"; the same is true of a "post-hole" in an ancient floor, which one school sees as symbolic of "a pupil in an iris" while the other "thinks a post-hole is a post-hole" (*HL*, 11).

The light, almost playful tone here would have been unthinkable in *North*, but here it indicates the development of a more complex position within his culture, and in terms of thinking about that culture. Here, though absent from the language of the poem, the "I" is very much the focus of the parable. Unlike the anguished figure in "Exposure", he can now comment on the "subversives and collaborators" who are always vying with each other "for the right to 'set the island story' straight" (*HL*, 11). These terms, analogous to the earlier "internee" and "informer", are viewed far more dispassionately, indicating his sense of distance from both positions.

In "From the Frontier of Writing" he again eschews the use of the "I" in a manner which makes it very different from an analogous poem in *Field Work*, entitled "The Toome Road". In both poems, there is an encounter with the British army, but in "The Toome Road", there is a palpable antagonism towards the "armoured cars": an antagonism flagged by the clear use of possessive pronouns: "How long were they approaching down my roads / As if they owned them?" (*FW*, 15). In "From the Frontier of Writing", however, there is no "I"; instead there is the colloquial "you" which ambiguously refers to both speaker and listener. The idea of absence, as opposed to the aggrieved presence of "The Toome Road", is stressed from the outset: "The tightness and nilness around that space" (*HL*, 6).

Much has been written about this poem, with Helen Vendler describing it in terms of structure, with "four opening tercets — in which the poet is stopped by a police roadblock" balanced by four "almost identical tercets" in which "the poet is self-halted, while writing, at the frontier of con-

science" (Vendler, 1998: 115). Daniel Tobin agrees, noting
the use of form of Dante's *terza rima* to describe a "political
and historical hell" as well as marking "a passage into the
purgatory of writing" (Tobin, 1998: 232), while Thomas Foster cites an interview with Heaney where the poet speaks
about this poem:

> Which uses an encounter at a roadblock, a kind of
> archetypal, Ulster, Catholic situation. It turns it into
> a parable for the inquisition and escape and freedom
> implicit in a certain kind of lyric poem. You know,
> you cross the bar and you're free into that other re-
> gion. (Foster, 1989: 132)

In a perceptive reading of this poem, and indeed of the later
poetry as a whole, Molino suggests that one of the most important aspects of this poetry is the exposure of the plurality of identification that constitutes the individual and collective consciousness (Molino, 1994: 190). I would agree, but
would make the further point that, when taken in context
with the thread of self-interrogation which we have been
exploring through his work, this poem enacts this very
process. As a parable, the poem takes a paradigmatic incident — the stopping of the "I" at a British army checkpoint,
and makes it turn back on itself in a parabolic arc so that it
becomes symbolic of the developing aesthetic which we
have been examining. Heaney has already written about being stopped at a checkpoint in "The Ministry of Fear" in
North, describing the "muzzle of a sten-gun in my eye" and
noting the reaction to his obviously Catholic name:

> "What's your name, driver?"
>   "Seamus . . ."
>   *Seamus?* (*N*, 64)

In the present poem, the frontier is seen as a liminal point, a
border which is a point of entry into a new dimension as

opposed to a form of blockage. Here, the checkpoint functions less as a political intrusion into the life of the individual
and more as a parable of the need for interrogation *by the
other* if the self is to achieve a form of transformation: "and
everything is pure interrogation" (*HL*, 6). Levinas terms this
questioning by the "presence of the Other, *ethics*" (Levinas,
1969: 43), and there is an increasing ethical strain to be
found in Heaney's work.

Here, the process instigated in "Digging" which has been
developed through "Exposure", the "Glanmore Sonnets"
and "Casualty", to cite some nodal points, is further developed by the image of the frontier of writing being seen as a
type of interrogative checkpoint, where the givens of selfhood, what Wilson Foster has called "the cultural becks and
calls" (Wilson Foster, 1995: 25), are subjected to interrogation. The value of the border as a point of self-questioning is
proof that such a complexity of perspective has been, to
some degree, achieved. The notion of being "arraigned yet
freed" is a powerful statement of the new perspective that
he has achieved in his traversing of the frontier of writing.

In the title poem, the notion of aesthetic distance is again
stressed as the "haw lantern", seen as a "small light for small
people", is transformed into the "roaming shape of Diogenes /
with his lantern, seeking one just man". This roaming figure in
search of some form of justice is also a trope of interrogation:
"so you end up scrutinized from behind the haw", and "you
flinch" before his gaze (*HL*, 7). Again, the pronoun is "you",
which both addresses and implicates the reader as well as
voiding the "I" of its immanent position.

In "The Stone Grinder", the personal pronoun does re-
appear but in a manner that is highly significant given our
discussion of the growth of the plurality of the identification
of which Molino spoke. As Peter McDonald has put it: "the
Heaney of the 1980s and after does not inhabit the discourses of identity in any very comfortable way" (McDonald,

1997: 12), and he goes on to cite this poem as an example. The stone grinder's work consists of preparing "old lithographs" by grinding "the same stones for fifty years", and whereas his work prepares the stones for "a new start and a clean slate", for him, it is a "coming full circle / like the ripple perfected in stillness" (HL, 8). It highlights Heaney's growing interest in the absences that form part of the self and of narrative in a "future of absences as well as presences" (McDonald, 1997: 13). This increasing focus on absence again locates Heaney in the realms of contemporary theory, where absence, or lack, as an index of subjectivity is a key tenet of the psychoanalytic theory of Jacques Lacan, who sees subjectivity as an endless process of dialectic between the self and the observing other.

In "From the Republic of Conscience", Heaney again stresses how much the sense of place and identity exists in the mind as opposed to in the land itself. However, despite the widely held view that these poems were something of a new departure, the patriarchal tradition is very much in evidence in the line where an old man "produced a wallet from his homespun coat" and "showed me a photograph of my grandfather". So, he is, in a sense, returning to the values of his own tradition, but those "curt cuts of an edge" appear here in terms of a disjointed, airy feel to the place, with no real sense that he is describing anything but a state of mind, where "You carried your own burden" (HL, 12). Here, those in power had to swear to uphold "the unwritten law" and they had to "weep / to atone for their presumption to hold office" (HL, 13). The speaker, called at different times, both "you" and "I", comes back from that "frugal republic" transformed, his customs "allowance" being himself, and he has now become a "dual citizen" who speaks on behalf of this republic in "his own tongue". The poem closes with the declaration that their embassies were "everywhere", but they operated independently and "no ambassador would ever be relieved" (*HL*, 13). It is as if he is describing a place which is both here and not here: a "now-here" and at the same time, a "no-where", and here I would disagree with Hart, who reads this poem directly in terms of Northern Irish politics (Hart, 1992: 197). It is significant, in this context, that the poem was written for Amnesty International. What happens here is far broader, as Heaney enunciates a new allegiance to the dictates of conscience and reason, an allegiance which acts as a counterweight to those appetites of gravity of which we have spoken.

In "From the Land of the Unspoken", he continues this process, as he refers to the "bar of platinum", in the International Bureau of Weights and Measures, near Paris, as a standard of measurement, and imagines himself "at home inside that metal core", an image which deconstructs much of his earlier poetic allegiance to the soil, both real and mythic, of his home territory. Home is now imaged in terms of a piece of metal in Paris, itself symbolic of a form of objectivity. As his poetry develops, he questions that "sensation of opaque fidelity" which his "dispersed people" take for their history, and the "legends" that have bound this people together (*HL*, 18). In this poem, there is a harsh critique of such "unspoken assumptions" which have the "force / of revelation":

> How else could we know
> that whoever is the first of us to seek
> assent and votes in a rich democracy
> will be the last of us and have killed our language? (*HL*, 19)

This poem, which could be reductively assessed in terms of measurement versus myth, stresses a different sense of home to that of the mythopoeic "assumptions" of his tradition. Here, he progresses along what he later terms his "*via negativa*" (*HL*, 51), in terms of an exploration of the "I".

In a very real sense, this process has much to do with the sequence "Clearances", in memory of his mother, who died in 1984. Here, in contradistinction to "Digging", he examines his maternal tradition, that of "The Exogamous Bride", his "great-grandmother's turncoat brow", through a "stone" that was thrown at her (*HL*, 25), moving forward in time to the "shining room" that was the "polished" splendour of his maternal grandmother's house (*HL*, 26), before finally, in the third sonnet, reaching his mother. Here, in a silent communion, paralleling the more formal, religious ceremony, while "the others were away at mass", he recalls himself and his mother silently peeling the potatoes: "I was all hers . . . Never closer the rest of our lives" (*HL*, 27).

It is in sonnet 7 that her death is described in terms of its effect on those in the room with her:

> That space we stood around had been emptied
> Into us to keep, it penetrated
> Clearances that suddenly stood open.
> High cries were felled and a pure change happened. (*HL*, 31)

Here, in his mother's death, the notion of space and absence as sources and as necessary aspects of identity are made clear. To return to "Digging", the physicality and materiality of the imagery of that poem is now counterbalanced by the maternal side of his tradition, a side which, in the silence of the relationship between son and mother, mirrors the silence of that aspect of his identity. In that early foundational poem, there was no mention of any women. Here, the silenced aspect has found its voice by inducting him into a new paradigm where absence and gap are valued. The knowledge arrived at here is: "poetic knowledge, an order of understanding capable of a sense of wholeness, an open O filled with attention" (Welch, 1992: 180).

In the closing sonnet, he refers to the "decked chestnut tree" which was cut down in Mossbawn, a tree which was his "coeval", planted by his aunt at his birth and associated with him. This image of rootedness would not have been out of place in the earlier books, but here, it is an image transformed, as he talks of walking "round and round a space / Utterly empty, utterly a source", and goes on to explain how presence had become absence, but an absence transformed: its "heft and hush become a bright nowhere, / . . . Silent, beyond silence listened for" (*HL*, 32).

In the final parable poem, "From the Canton of Expectation", he traces the history of Northern Ireland through a parable of grammar: the "optative moods" of the early generations of nationalists, playing their "rebel anthem", followed by a "grammar / of imperatives" as a new generation pave and pencil "their first causeways / across the prescribed texts" (*HL*, 46). This generation would "banish the conditional forever", seeing little value in the ethic of endurance that was espoused by the older generation. In the final section, he writes of a return of the repressed, as the virtues of a past age under "the guardian angel of passivity" now "sink a fang of menace" in his shoulder. He has come full circle, seeing the reaction of his own tribe as menacing, given his broader perspective of vision in the last books. The poem concludes, not with tribal affirmation but with a return to the optative mood of the opening line, as he yearns for "one among us" who never swerved from what "all his instincts told him was right action", and who, in keeping with the grammatical structure of the poem "stood his ground in the indicative" (*HL*, 47). Once more, there is a shift from group to individual. As Molino perceptively notes, such a person would be ready for the "profound prospects of change" (Molino, 1994: 184), though the poem seems to be in no way optimistic in its view of those changes.

"The Mud Vision", the "strongest and strangest poem in *The Haw Lantern*" (Corcoran, 1998: 153), is a poem where a communal vision of change is offered, and rejected. It describes what could well be contemporary Ireland, with its mixture of "punks" and the "last of the mummers", and its walking the line between "panic and formulae". He captures the sense of change that has taken place in the country, and also the sense that people are looking for something in which to believe, having seen their old icons gradually lose their gilt. Heaney's original source was a display of concentric circles, each made of muddy "hand prints" by the artist Richard Long (Heaney, 1996: 10). The vision, coming as a moment of quasi-transcendent certainty in a world full of change and uncertainty, is nevertheless qualified, its source being fore-grounded: "A gossamer wheel, concentric with its own hub / Of nebulous dirt, sullied yet lucent". As a vision, it is singularly dirty: "sunsets ran murky" and car wipers were unable to "entirely clean off the windscreen" (*HL*, 48). He speaks of a "generation who had seen a sign" (*HL*, 49) and describes this sign in terms that are familiar to readers of *North*, as "if a rose window of mud" had invented itself (*HL*, 48).

In "Exposure", he felt that he had missed the portent, whereas now, the "sign" has appeared in the midst of the present. The nature of the sign, its materiality, is different from that of the "comet's pulsing rose" in "Exposure" (*N*, 73), which came from above, so to speak. Here, the "vision" is part of the stuff that has been the elemental material of Heaney's own writing: clay, earth, mud. In ways, this "vision" could refer to his own visionary aspects of land and belonging, and the quasi-religious tenor of the imagery — "a smudge on their foreheads", and "altars" where "bulrushes ousted the lilies" (*HL*, 48) — calls to mind the phenomenon of the "moving statues" in Ireland in the late 1970s and early 1980s, where groups of people saw signs of movement in statues located in outdoor altars and shrines.

The desire for some "sign" that would make everything clear has been enunciated in Heaney's own writing, and here, it is given voice in the plural as people are bound together by their common sense of the vision before them: "only ourselves / Could be adequate then to our lives" (*HL*, 49). However, it disappeared as suddenly as it had appeared: "One day it was gone", and the remainder of the poem discusses the "*post factum* jabber" that ensued (*HL*, 49). Corcoran makes the telling points that this poem could serve as an allegory of the revolutionary fervour of Irish independence which ossified into a reactionary Catholic nationalism, or else to the civil rights movement of the late 1960s in Northern Ireland, where a genuine new beginning seemed possible, only to result in thirty years of attritional violence between the two communities (Corcoran, 1998: 153–4). In starkly political terms, this is a fine reading, but possibly there is a more generalised point at issue here.

In *North*, the sign was seen as a portent, something which would free him from indecision, something which Heaney has "missed" in "Exposure"; here, the sign is seen as a *chimera*, as non-existent: it is created from the very stuff of the earth, "mud" and returns to that elemental stuff. As he puts it: "What might have been origin / We dissipated in news", and goes on to make the telling comment that the "clarified place" had retrieved "neither us nor itself" except "You could say we survived" (*HL*, 49). The more mature Heaney now sees "signs" and "visions" with a more jaundiced eye: he has "second thoughts" about the very nature of the visionary, seeing it as no longer something to be caught and venerated. Instead, he now sees visions as experiences to be survived. Rather than look for huge manifestations and visions, his aesthetic is now more keenly attuned to seeing the visionary in the ordinary, but it is a more personalised vision, with "I" being used far more often than the vatic or tribal "we". Worn down by years of violence in Northern Ireland, and bombs in England and mainland Europe, the given republicanism of many people in the Republic of Ireland had undergone a similar fate: the vision of a united Ireland was being unpacked, and the nationalist card remained unplayed in elections. Similarly, the hegemonic position of the Catholic church began to decline, in the wake of a number of sexual scandals. The twin pillars of a communal sense of Irishness — republicanism and Catholicism — were in decline, and Heaney's increased focus on the personal is a significant index of this situation.

In this phase of his work, allusions, both immediate and sustained, to works of European culture become more prevalent, as his use of Dante's *terza rima* (stanzas of three lines) in "Squarings" indicates. *Seeing Things* is framed by translations of two of the cornerstones of European literature, Virgil's *Aeneid* and Dante's *Inferno*, thereby setting the tone for a work that combines the quotidian with the literary. Bernard O'Donoghue makes the telling point that this book "remains intent on thresholds and crossings throughout its formally very different parts", citing the title of the Dante translation, "Crossings", as emblematic of the book itself (O'Donoghue, 1994: 120).

As the previous book was about "second thoughts", so this one is about seeing things anew — a second look where things are seen in their full complexity. Classical art is the prism through which this new and differential perspective can be brought to bear on the process of "seeing". The vision involved here is very different from that of "The Mud Vision". There, vision was a single, communal act, sanctioned by the group; here, it is an ongoing process of transformation, which takes place within the consciousness of the individual. The title phrase also encompasses another sense of "seeing things": the "imagining of what is not literally there" (O'Donoghue, 1994: 123).

Personal grief at the death of his father is one of the dominant tropes of this book, with the opening translation, through the voice of Aeneas, allowing him to look for "one face-to-face meeting with my dear father" in a verbal context where "clear

truths and mysteries / Were inextricably twined" (*ST*, 1). The
desire to escape from this world to some form of other-world
is strong, but the familiar sense of obligation and duty is also
present: "But to retrace your steps and get back to upper air, /
This is the real task and the real undertaking" (*ST*, 2). For
Heaney, no vision, be it mud or other-world, can provide an
escape from his sense of obligation to write about the world
as it is and as he sees it, no matter how uncomfortable that
may make him, or his audience.

His sense of complex vision is crystallised in "The Journey Back" where Dante and Philip Larkin are juxtaposed.
Corcoran makes the point that, just as Heaney made the
shade of Joyce Heaney-like in *Station Island*, so here, Larkin
assumes aspects of Heaney's poetic personality (Corcoran,
1998: 164). Douglas Dunn makes much the same point, noting that while it is meant to be Larkin speaking, "it sounds
too much like Heaney" (Dunn, 2001: 210). It is not that
Larkin is speaking: rather is it that Heaney is using the spectral Larkin as a thickening device to develop his own poetic
persona. The journey back here is a direct consequence of
the previous poem, where he desired to escape from this
world to another; now, he is: "like the forewarned journey
back / Into the heartland of the ordinary". This is Larkin
seen through the prism of Dante: "*to face / The ordeal of my
journey and my duty*" (*ST*, 7) [*italics original*], and it is also
Heaney, facing his duty to journey alone in a world where
both parents have died. There is no visionary certainty here;
only the insights brought about by imagination.

Such insights are the concern of "markings", as the archetypal "four jackets for four goalposts" delineates a childhood football game; in itself, nothing out of the ordinary.
However, in a stylistic device that is paradigmatic of this
book's, and indeed the later Heaney's, methodology, as the
"light died" they kept on playing because "by then they were
playing in their heads", as some "limit had been passed" (*ST*,

8). The passing of limits is at the core of Heaney's later work, as the power of the imagination to alter the "givens" of reality has become a seminal preoccupation in his writing. Here, the transformation from the actual to the imagined is repeated in different contexts, the already discussed football game, the "lines pegged out" in a garden, or in the "outline of a house foundation" (*ST*, 8), which metamorphose into "the imaginary line straight down". This transforming of the very essence of foundation into the imaginary symbolises the "pure change" that has been the latest dimension of his work. In the third section, the transforming power of these markings, initially physical but changed into the imaginative, has the function of blurring the traditional categories of grammar. Here, the transfigurative power of such imaginative markings is made overt:

> All these things entered you
> As if they were both the door and what came through it.
> They marked the spot, marked time and held it open. (*ST*, 9)

At this juncture, we have the opening of the "I" to all aspects of experience, an opening that foreshadows the opening of the Irish psyche in the 1990s, as a more cosmopolitan sense of identity began to take shape in the country. The final image of the poem reinforces this transformative aspect of writing, as two men sawing a "felled beech" seemed to "row the steady earth" (*ST*, 9). These images of transformation brought about through the act of writing are synecdochic of the later Heaney. No longer feeling the need or "duty" to speak for his tribal and group identity, he now probes the limits that are passed through creative imagination, a process which can have salutary effects on the sense of selfhood. As O'Donoghue puts it, such crossings are central, and language is "the most universal crossing of all, because transference of meaning — 'translation' — is its very nature", and he sees the poem as mirroring the Saussurean idea of the arbitrariness of language (O'Donoghue, 1994: 121).

This ability to "see things" in a new linguistic light permeates the book as a whole. In "Casting and Gathering", he begins with a statement that is redolent of his earlier, politically contextualised work: "Years and years ago, these sounds took sides", and continues with a change of tense, from past to present, and a change of perspective: "I have grown older and can see them both" and concludes with a re-vision of the initial binarism: "For I see that when one man casts, the other gathers / And then *vice versa*, without changing sides" (*ST*, 13). The idea of taking one side over the other is seen as childish: the more mature perspective is more tolerant. His changed perspective allows him to eschew monumental visions for the more microcosmic ones "Blessed be down-to-earth" (*ST*, 14). Here, the "pure change" that has occurred is in the mind of the perceiver, who can use imagination to transform the "down-to-earth" into some form of revelation.

In the title poem, "Seeing Things", he speaks of a boat trip to Inishbofin, and foregrounds the crossing between land and island as the most important aspect of the journey:

> What guaranteed us —
> That quick response and buoyancy and swim —
> Kept me in agony. (*ST*, 16)

The significance of the journey is precisely the "agony" of the uncertain movement that guaranteed progress from mainland to island. Symbolically, this suggests that his new sense of "seeing" focuses on the very nature of process as opposed to product: as he puts it in *Crediting Poetry*: "poetic form is both the ship and the anchor" (*CP*, 29) and this is an important image of his changing perspective. Tobin makes the relevant point that this poem has echoes of the two classical translations which frame the book, adding that the detail contributes to the image of the journey as "an allegory of the poet's own risky passage" (Tobin, 1998: 269).

This imaginative process is also the subject of "Field of Vision", where he describes a woman who "sat for years", looking "straight ahead". This sense of looking is admired by the speaker of the poem, as he comments on looking "across a well-braced gate" and discovering that:

> the field behind the hedge
> Grew more distinctly strange as you kept standing
> Focused and drawn in by what barred the way. (*ST*, 22)

Once more, he sees beyond the real and, like so many other poems in this book, there is a connection with the theory of *ostranenie*, defamiliarisation or making strange, coined by the Russian Formalist critics. Victor Shklovsky made the point that perception is often dulled by the force of habit; it becomes automatic and dull, and all sense of any new sensation is lost. Art, says Shklovsky, exists "that one may recover the sensation . . . it exists to make one feel things, to make the stone *stony*" (Shklovsky, 1965: 12). Thus, to see the field in a new way is to look at it through the gate, to examine the process of connection between the two. Heaney's sense of defamiliarisation by looking at the processes of perception is pervasive in this book, as he "sees things" in a unique way. Thus the "perfection" of a "pitchfork" is described in terms of its "imagined perfection"; this, in turn, is described, not in terms of the object itself, but in terms of the "opening hand" which reached out for it (*ST*, 23).

Perhaps the apotheosis of this trope in the book is to be found in "A Basket of Chestnuts". This poem is about the portrait of Heaney, painted by Edward Maguire in 1973, which appeared on the back of the original printing of *North*. It has Heaney sitting at a table, reading a book, and looking straight out at the viewer. One would expect the usual adjectivally strong, detailed description of the chestnuts. However, the poem begins with what he terms a "shadow-boost", a "giddy strange assistance / That happens when you swing a loaded basket". He goes on to describe that defamiliarising process again, as he outlines the "lightness" that inheres in the weight as the basket reaches the limit of its upswing: "your hands feel unburdened, / Outstripped, dismayed, passed through" and then "comes rebound — Downthrust and comeback ratifying you" (*ST*, 24). This delight in the ordinary, and in the process of remembering that basket of chestnuts, is ratified by his discussion of the dialectic of heaviness and lightness, and more specifically of the effects of both: both are seen to be of value, both are seen as the image of each other, and this sense of wholeness of experience is one of the "things" most clearly "seen" in this book.

However, there is another layer of meaning in this poem. This specific basket was to feature as an aspect of the portrait which Maguire would eventually paint of Heaney. Thus, it "shines between" Heaney and Maguire, even though it remained unpainted: "But it wasn't in the picture and is not" (*ST*, 24). As the poem coheres in the final stanza, the image of the shadow-boost takes on a broader tenor: what is in the picture is "comeback, especially for him" (referring to Maguire), while:

> the basket shines and foxfire chestnuts gleam
> Where he passed through, unburdened and dismayed.
> (*ST*, 25)

The repetition of the terms used about the basket in the opening two stanzas, but here referring to the painter and Heaney, the two artists who, in their different ways, "see things" anew, is telling. The chestnuts, absent from the portrait, are present in the poem: the "shadow-boost" and "rebound" enact the sense of complexity and wholeness that has become the most significant part of Heaney's developing aesthetic sense. The ability to reimagine the past, to make

present that which was absent, and to make real that which
does not exist, has become hugely important to Heaney in
terms of how and why he writes.

This is an individual sensibility tracing its own development, a process symbolised in "Hailstones":

> I made a small hard ball
> of burning water running from my hand
>
> just as I make this now
> out of the melt of the real thing
> smarting into its absence. (*HL*, 14)

This dialectic of presence and absence gives him a structure
with which to deal with the historical, traditional and socio-
cultural "givens" which have long exercised a gravitational
pull on his work. In "The Settle Bed", this new-found sense
of freedom is applied to both his early family home, and
then, in that dialectical fashion which has been very much a
modus operandi of this book, to his broader political and religious homeland.

The poem begins in classical Heaney fashion with a heavily adjectival description of an object, made of "seasoned
deal / Dry as the unkindled boards of a funeral ship" (*ST*, 28).
The simile, immediately redolent of the Viking atmosphere
of *North*, harks back to that early period of Heaney's writing,
but in a manner which underlines the fact that "Heaney's
work does not stay still" (Cookson and Dale, 1989: 3), as
the solidity of the bed, redolent of the seeming solidity of
Heaney's earlier tribal and group identifications, is gradually
altered. As a "thing" from the past, the bed is full of echoes
of "the long bedtime / anthems of Ulster", and again, we appear to be inhabiting the territory of *North*, where physical
and material items conjured up ideologies of belonging and
territorial piety. Here, in keeping with the altered perspective, this bed conjures up aspects of both communities:

"Protestant, Catholic, the Bible, the beads", as he attempts to locate himself in the broader context of his heritage.

Of course, the very definitions of these two communities are themselves readings of different cultural items from the past, a reading that places these in a narrative which, in turn, defines Catholics in terms of the rosary beads, and Protestants in terms of the Bible. As in *North*, he is dealing with notions of a cultural and traditional inheritance, and he makes this point specifically in the fourth stanza:

> And now this is "an inheritance" —
> Upright, rudimentary, unshiftably planked
> In the long ago, yet willable forward
>
> Again and again and again . . .
> And un-get-roundable weight. (*ST*, 28)

One could see the inheritances of both Northern and Southern Ireland in this light. In Northern Ireland, the inheritances of communal strife, religious and political intolerance, allied to a historically sanctioned sense of grievance, have remained formidable forces in the present, while in the Republic of Ireland, the hegemonic forces of nationalism and Catholicism have been dominant since the inception of the state.

The notion of an "inheritance" being "willable forward" can be seen to permeate contemporary Irish social and political life on both sides of the border. As Catharine Malloy puts it, what is happening here is the initiation of "new dialogues that influence the old, dormant, suspended ones, freeing them from immutability by inviting a gathering of new discourses to assist him in redressing a past event" (Malloy, 1996: 158). Heaney himself has been subject to the gravitational pull and attachments of such notions of inheritance, as we saw from the outset in "Digging". Here, he sees such an inheritance as a "weight" which pulls people downward. However, in the context of the preoccupation with process and dialectic that we have been tracing throughout this book in particular, the poem will set out a counter-movement which will, in a manner similar to that discussed in "A Basket of Chestnuts", act as a counter-weight, a "shadow-boost" to that weight. In this poem, his strategy involves imagining a "dower of settle beds" tumbling from heaven.

Interestingly, he compares this imagined barrage of settle beds to "some nonsensical vengeance come on the people" (*ST*, 29), a comment which ironically revisits his earlier notions of understanding the "exact and / tribal, intimate revenge" (*N*, 38), and of seeming to validate the idea of "slaughter / for the common good" (*N*, 45). Communal vengeance, itself an inheritance from the past, can drag the present into the mire of sectarianism. Here "political anachronism and the atavisms of both sides" are "lightened or loosened" (Corcoran, 1998: 172) by this "shadow-boost" and the all-important "pure change" is flagged in the seventh stanza, as people learn:

> from that harmless barrage that whatever is given

> Can always be reimagined, however four-square,
> Plank-thick, hull-stupid and out of its time
> It happens to be. (*ST*, 29)

It is this reimagining of the past that is the key to this poem, and by extension, to this book. Just as his personal past, in terms of Maguire's portrait, was reimagined through the image of the basket of chestnuts, so, Heaney seems to be saying, the political past can be reimagined so that the inheritance can be redrawn in an image that is coherent and in tune with its own time. The image of a parallel settle bed of the imagination harkens to the imagined basket of chestnuts and to the other boat "sailing through the air" of "Seeing Things".

The purpose of writing, it would seem, for Heaney, is now to enable and ratify this process of transformation, of "pure change". This is clear from the "Glanmore Revisited" sequence, where the introspection and questioning of the "Glanmore Sonnets" of *Field Work* is replaced by a new calmness and surety of his poetic vocation, "an old / Rightness half-imagined or foretold" (*ST*, 31). No longer self-conscious about his "apology for poetry" (*FW*, 41), he can now speak of Glanmore as "the same *locus amoenus*" (*ST*, 32), and can tell that he is able to "swim in Homer" (*ST*, 36). Whereas before he was questioning the role of the poet in terms of his or her cultural affiliations and givens, now he is increasingly aware of the "book of changes" that writing allows him to create: "Who ever saw / The limit in the given anyhow?" (*ST*, 46). The inheritances of the past can be changed, reimagined, redrawn in order to become more of a source than a hindrance, a source of the marvellous as well as of the malign:

> And poetry
> Sluggish in the doldrums of what happens.
> Me waiting until I was nearly fifty
> To credit marvels. (*ST*, 50)

In the second section of the book, the "Squarings" sequence "cumulates into a long poem of 576 lines in four equal parts" (Dunn, 2001: 220). This sequence, itself the culmination of a generic tendency that reaches back to "A Lough Neagh Sequence" in *Door into the Dark*, is part of a continuing experiment with form, an effort that attempts to find a form that will combine "the fluid and the phantomatic", an experiment which will be continued in his prose. This form consists of "forty-eight twelve-liners, each of the poems arranged in four unrhymed tercets in freely handled iambic pentameter" which can be seen as a looser version of Dante's *terza rima* (Andrews, 1998: 156). The sequence is full of those mo-

ments of attention to process and movement which can de-
familiarise the quotidian so fully that it become the stuff of
vision and change. In the opening section, "Lightenings", he
speaks of "Shifting brilliancies" (*ST*, 55), of "Test-outs and
pull-backs, re-envisagings" (*ST*, 57), of the "music of the arbi-
trary" (*ST*, 59), of Thomas Hardy's imagining "himself a
ghost" and of how he "circulated with that new perspective"
(*ST*, 61). He poses the question, redolent of so much of this
book, of whether one could "reconcile / What was diapha-
nous there with what was massive?" (*ST*, 64).

The second section, "Settings" is equally full of such defamiliarising visions of the ordinary, expressed in terms of
process, journey and dialectic:

> whatever was in store
> Witnessed itself already taking place
> In a time marked by assent and by hiatus. (*ST*, 70)

This encompassing poetic continues: "I stood in the door,
unseen and blazed upon" (*ST*, 71) stresses his ability to inhabit different aspects of an opposition through the process
of moving freely between them. In an *hommage* to Yeats's
"What Then", he poses the core question: "Where does
spirit live? Inside or outside / Things remembered, made
things, things unmade?" (*ST*, 78), while the second section
concludes with a poem that harks back to "Lovers on Aran"
in *Death of a Naturalist*, where "Sea broke on land to full
identity" (*DON*, 47), as he writes of "Air and ocean" as
"antecedents / of each other", going on to define this relationship as "Omnipresence" and "equilibrium" (*ST*, 80).

In "Crossings", the third section, this theme of process
and dialectic is further developed, as "Everything flows" (*ST*,
85), and moments of clarity are found wherein a "pitch" is
reached beyond "our usual hold upon ourselves" (*ST*, 86).
He talks of a "music of binding and of loosing" (*ST*, 87), and
exemplifies this through speaking of "a meaning made of

trees. / Or not exactly trees" (ST, 89), while in the final section, he invokes poems by "the sage Han Shan", who is able
to write about a place "Cold Mountain", and refer, at the
same time to:

> a place that can also mean
> A state of mind. Or different states of mind
>
> At different times. (ST, 97)

Here we see the results of the "Lightenings", "Settings" and
"Crossings" that have led to this final section, "Squarings", of
the sequence as a whole. The given, set notion of place and
tradition — a notion heavily interlinked with language, naming and what he later terms "cold memory-weights / To load
me, hand and foot, in the scale of things" (ST, 100) (which
seems to hearken back to the "un-get-roundable weight" of
"Settle Bed") — is now set in a fluid relationship which both
"lightens" and allows for "crossings" in an architectonic
structure which has room for the traditional notion of place,
and at the same time for transformative notions of that
place. One can go on to extrapolate ideas of identity and
politics from this, as Heaney sets out his structure of four
groups of twelve poems, each composed of twelve lines, or
four groups of three lines. The numerological complexity
serves as a paradigm of the increasing complexity of his
work specifically in terms of notions of identity, and the
transformations that can take place therein. These transformations parallel the increasingly complex political and social
structures that were coming into being in the Ireland of the
time, with religious, social and cultural practices becoming
more fluid and plural, and less predefined.

The increasingly European and American influences on
Irish culture have broadened our comparative and contras-
tive sense of self, a process which is at the core of Heaney's
own project. We have seen his development from the im-

manent voice of his own tribe, and the attempt to voice a sense of the identity of that tribe, to a more individualistic probing of the constituents of his own expanding sense of self, a sense which has become increasingly permeated by the voices of other cultures and other languages.

This individual process has its societal analogue in the increasing sense of Ireland as a country within Europe, which also has strong ties to the American Anglophone world, as opposed to the old binary oppositional relationship with Britain. As a culture, it would seem, we have now come to define ourselves less in terms of our history, and more in terms of our geographical placement. The recent economic successes of the oft-cited Celtic Tiger have given a new sense of confidence, but paradoxically, it was through a more culturally and economically expansionist mindset that this phenomenon came into being in the first place. Heaney's later work moves away from the soil-obsessed earlier artesian probings, and instead, looks outward into other languages and cultures in its attempt to define a sense of developing selfhood.

All of this harks back to the idea, propounded in "Squarings", that a place can mean a "state of mind" or indeed "different states of mind / At different times". This process of decentring of place and of the certainties that pertained to such notions of place has profound implications for the historical narrative of Irish republicanism, a narrative which has been hard-wired into Heaney's system and which his ongoing poetic project has attempted to disconnect, to some degree. In *The Spirit Level*, as well as his translations, *The Cure at Troy*, *The Midnight Verdict*, *The Burial at Thebes* and his collaborative translation of Jan Kochanowski's *Laments*, the otherness that is a necessary part of all attempts to define an Irishness that is increasingly part of a European and American dialectical influence will be explored.

Chapter Four

A Different Shore

Part of the development of Heaney's work is to be found in an ever-increasing use of classical reference. We have already seen how *Seeing Things* is framed by the *Aeneid* and the *Divina Comedia*, and the final poem of that book, "The Crossing" makes concrete the developing theme of transformation and translation that we have been examining throughout this period of his work. In this poem, the speaker, Dante originally, but in this case Heaney too, is refused entry into the underworld by Charon the ferryman, a refusal that his guide, Virgil, sees as an indication of his virtue:

> No good spirits ever pass this way
> And therefore, if Charon objects to you,
> You should understand well what his words imply. (*ST*, 113)

Here, at the close of a volume in which "most of the poems before it describe crossings" (Andrews, 1998: 160), the point is made that descent into the underworld, symbolic of a descent into the world of death and the past, is not for everyone. Whereas poetry allows for a voicing of the dead, and for the presence of the past, it also, in ethical terms, upholds notions of goodness that are at a higher level than those of the underworld, where "fear is turned into desire"

(*ST*, 112). It would, however, be wrong to see this volume as ending on a note of limitation. Instead, what is stressed here is that a passage into the underworld, itself symbolic of the earlier tribal artesian imperative, is no longer compatible with Heaney's developing ethical sense of the value of poetry in society and culture. It is not that his crossing is blocked; rather is it redirected by Charon:

> He said, "By another way, by other harbours
> You shall reach a different shore and pass over.
> A lighter boat must be your carrier." (*ST*, 111)

This "lighter boat" and the implied destination of a "different shore" symbolise the process that Heaney has been undergoing in his work as he attempts to bring into question the givens of tradition and identity that have been his lot. The ethical aspect of poetry has always been an implication of his work, but in these later books, it becomes more overt. Through his use of classical imagery, he is able to achieve a new perspective on his own situation so that he can write about issues that affect him deeply, while at the same time achieving a measure of distance. We recall the use of Tacitus in "Kinship" to achieve this end, and in his next translation, *The Cure at Troy*, classical imagery of a destructive war, and an ensuing demand for tribal vengeance, is used to achieve a crossing from the tribal to the ethical.

In *The Cure at Troy*, he "face[s] the music" in terms of his nationalist heritage by attempting to find a position which transcends the binarism of nationalist and unionist. The translation is a version of Sophocles' *Philoctetes*, written for Field Day, and first produced in October of 1990 in the Guildhall in Derry. The premise of the translation is clear. Philoctetes, a Greek hero, has been "dumped" on the island of Lemnos by the Greek army due to his "cankered foot" (*CT*, 3). This wounded foot, caused by a "snake-bite he got at a shrine" (*CT*, 17), caused him to break into "howling fits"

(*CT*, 3) which was putting the Greeks "on edge", and making everybody's nerves "raw" (*CT*, 4); hence their decision to abandon him. However, Philoctetes had inherited the "actual bow and arrows" that had belonged to Hercules (*CT*, 17).

Significantly, according to a Trojan soothsayer, Helenus, one of King Priam's sons, Troy would only be captured if Philoctetes and his bow were present. Hence the plot of the play as Odysseus and the hero of the play, Neoptolemus (the son of Achilles), are sent to obtain the bow, though this task is really a setting for an exploration of the conflicting demands of tribal loyalty and some form of higher notion of ethics. The drama enacts a process of crossing from one shore to the other, as the tribal is held in the balance against the ethical, and found wanting. The work is successful, as Patrick Crotty puts it, in "making the wound of Philoctetes emblematic of the trauma of Ulster's maimed and distrustful communities" (Crotty, 2001: 204).

The analogue between the classical *milieu* of the play and contemporary Northern Ireland is implied throughout, and made overt in the following lines from the chorus:

> The innocent in goals
> Beat on their bars together.
> A hunger-striker's father
> Stands in the graveyard dumb.
> The police widow in veils
> Faints at the funeral home. (*CT*, 77)

This sequence, coming close to the end of the play, "encourages allegorical readings" (Corcoran, 1998: 188), and causes the readers to retrospectively make connections between the situation of Neoptolemus, Philoctetes and Odysseus, and that of contemporary Northern Ireland. The demands of one's group are seen, at least in the eyes of Odysseus, to supersede those of any higher form of inter-subjective justice or ethics. The play traces the development of Neoptolemus from this position through moments of conflict and self-questioning, until he reaches a position beyond such views.

He begins as someone who, when told "you're here to serve our cause" replies unquestioningly: "What are the orders" (*CT*, 6). His unquestioning attitude to authority parallels that of an earlier Ireland to the twin authorities of church and state, and his notion of "us" is very narrow, and defined, as is that of Odysseus, in contrast to that of a similarly narrowly comprised "them". He undertakes the task — the commandeering of the bow from Philoctetes — and sets out to win the trust of the latter: "We're Greeks, so, all right, we do our duty" (*CT*, 8). However, through subtle use of textual and graphematic structure, Heaney indicates the levels of doubt that are increasingly a part of Neoptolemus's development. The falling line indicates a disjunction between the words spoken and the level of complicity between these words, between the political imperative that underwrites them and the individual consciousness that speaks them. The following examples indicate this process:

> Well then.
> > So be it.
> > > The weapons are our target. (*CT*, 10)

> Duplicity! Complicity!
> > All right.
> > > I'll do it. (*CT*, 11)

The parallel between Philoctetes and the communities in Northern Ireland gradually unfolds through the text, in phrases like: "their whole life spent admiring themselves / For their own long-suffering" (*CT*, 2) and "Every day has been a weeping wound" (*CT*, 19). The ties of family and those appetites of gravity are also present, ties with which Heaney too, as we have seen, is only too familiar:

> There was the Greek cause, and —
>   Inevitably —
> There was my father. (*CT*, 21)

The role of art is also interrogated, as the tale of the merchant, Odysseus's man in disguise, is told in order to further trick Philoctetes. In a way it is the art of the "hero / On some muddy compound" of "Exposure"; it is an art for "the people" (*N*, 72–3). However, its definition of "the people" is narrow and tribal: it is Greek art with a Greek purpose: it is art in the service of a cause: "Greeks with a job to do" (*CT*, 3). It is an art with a message, a message which reinforces the barriers between self and other as opposed to breaking them down: "But you'll be fit to read between the lines / For the message, whatever the message is" (*CT*, 11).

However, while this may be one use for art in the face of conflict, it is not the only one, as Neoptolemus gradually discovers. His growing sense that what he is doing is wrong, having already been mimetically indicated by the falling, broken line structure, is now developed thematically in the play as he touches the bow. Far from seeing this as a joyful and triumphalist climax to a plan of campaign, Neoptolemus responds thoughtfully to Philoctetes' comment that the touch is an example of the "generous behaviour" which got him the bow in the first place:

> There's a whole economy of kindness
> Possible in the world; befriend a friend
> And the chance of it's increased and multiplied. (*CT*, 37)

On getting the chance to steal the bow from the sleeping Philoctetes, Neoptolemus refuses, making the point that while "we could steal away with the bow" that would be "easy and meaningless". He also refuses the siren voices of pragmatism and *realpolitik* as enunciated by the chorus, who tell him that oracles are "devious", and that they don't "enquire too deep" into the ethics of such actions, as chances "like this / You can't afford to miss" (*CT*, 46).

Nevertheless, the appetites of gravity still exert their pull on him, and when Philoctetes asks for the bow to be returned, Neoptolemus makes the constrained reply: "I'm under orders" (*CT*, 51). The further shore towards which Neoptolemus is travelling throughout this play beckons more insistently when Philoctetes sums up the sense of ethical responsibility that he sees in the young man who knows that this:

> Solidarity with the Greeks is sham.
> The only real thing is the thing he lives for:
> His own self-respect. (*CT*, 53)

Here, the whole weight of the text is behind the onus on the individual to take personal responsibility. It is a position which we saw the Heaney of "Exposure" tease out, and there are analeptic textual connections with that poem in the language of Neoptolemus at this crucial juncture of the play: "How did I end up here? Why did I go / Behind backs ever" (*CT*, 53), recalls similar lines — "How did I end up like this" and "For what is said behind-backs" (*N*, 72–3) — of "Exposure". It is through this process of exposing himself to the idea of the other as an other person, requiring the same degrees of consideration as the self, that we can begin to see outside of our tribal walls.

It is this exposure that causes Neoptolemus to cry:

> I'm all throughother.
> > This isn't me.
> > > I'm sorry. (*CT*, 48)

What this means is that his sense of self has become permeated with a sense of responsibility to the other. Rather than defining himself in contradistinction to alterity, he sees it as part of him. As Levinas puts it, one is "defined as a subjectivity, as an 'I' precisely because one is exposed to the other" (Levinas: 1981; 62), and this is precisely what is at stake here. Thus he is in total contrast to the mindset of Odysseus (from whom I quote *seriatim*), whose perspective on identity is very far from a further shore:

> We were Greeks with a job to do . . .
> It worked so what about it? . . . (*CT*, 65)
>   The will of the Greek people,
> And me here as their representative . . . (*CT*, 66)
> You've turned yourself into a Trojan, lad,
> And that will have consequences. (*CT*, 67)

The final quote embodies dramatic irony in that these consequences will be a liberating function of art to transform the borders and boundaries of identity, through a focus on future possibilities as opposed to past entrenchments. This transformative potential is further embodied in the voice of the translation. As Molino puts it, and I would agree, Heaney here speaks through a co-opted "Sophoclean voice, resulting simultaneously in a familiarized and de-familiarized voice, a sense of the immediacy of and the distance from the experience of the play" (Molino, 1994, 127).

Heaney's poetic investment in this translation is hinted at in the number of submerged references to his own work that appear. We have already noted the linear similarity with "Exposure" and that poem's title appears in the line: "slow death by exposure" (*CT*, 59). Other titles and lines appear in hortatory lines from the play which focus on the transforming power of ethics and art:

> If you seek justice, you should deal justly always.
> You should *govern your tongue* and present a true
> case [*my italics*] (*CT*, 61)

> Stop just licking your wounds. Start *seeing things* [*my italics*] (*CT*, 74)

> Believe that *a further shore* / Is reachable from here [*my italics*] (*CT*, 77)

This notion of a "further shore", already adverted to in "The Crossing" as a different shore, inhabits much of Heaney's writing. It embodies the desire to find a different route to a different destination, a destination that offers new possibilities. As he puts it in the opening poem of *The Spirit Level*, when listening to a "rain stick", what happens next is "a music that you never would have known / To listen for" (*SL*, 1).

The breadth and scope of allusion in *The Spirit Level* enables this previously unheard music. In "To a Dutch Potter in Ireland", he speaks of the place of art in a broader conflict — the Netherlands of the Second World War — and again, it is the transformative that draws him in. He makes the connection between writing and pottery, where "*words like urns that had come through the fire*" can "*come away changed*" (*SL*, 2) [*italics original*]. Again, the poem is a translation of work, from the Dutch poet J.C. Bloem, and it provides that outward-looking perspective that has become such a central tenet of his developing aesthetic. As John Goodby and Ivan Phillips note:

> Sketching a series of parallels and contrasts . . . the poem sets out to locate the alchemical moment where the earthbound, whether clay or language, consciousness or history, is transformed "*in a diamond blaze of air*". (Goodby and Phillips, 2001: 246) [*italics original*]

The notion of process and of reaching towards distant shores is again the subject of "A Sofa in the Forties", a poem which treats material that is also the kernel of his Nobel Prize Lecture, *Crediting Poetry*. Here he speaks of a family sofa which, through childish imagination, was transformed: "for this was a train", and thence something that could achieve "Flotation" (*SL*, 7). The sofa becomes a paradigm of his own work, and of the Irish cultural psyche as it is "Potentially heavenbound" but "earthbound for sure" (*SL*, 8). A further imaginative transformation took place on that sofa "under the wireless shelf", as it was here that Heaney first heard voices from beyond, from further, different shores, be they the "*Yippee-i-ay*" of the "Riders of the Range" or the news, read by "the absolute speaker". This voice, probably the clipped English of a BBC newsreader, is significant as between "him and us" a "great gulf was fixed where pronunciation / Reigned tyrannically" (*SL*, 8). However, this gulf provided the opportunity for yet another "crossing", as, brought in by the "aerial wire", this "sway of language and its furtherings" allowed him to enter "history and ignorance" (*SL*, 8) and be "transported" (*SL*, 9).

Imagination has the ability to facilitate such transportation, but it cannot elide the dangers of Northern Ireland. In two poems dealing with family members — "Keeping Going" is dedicated to his brother Hugh, while "Two Lorries" recalls his mother — he stresses the almost casually normal nature of the violence in Northern Ireland, from the perspective of those who "stay on where it happens" (*SL*, 12). In a poem whose form enacts the image from "Sweeney Redivivus", of a "ball of wet twine" which was "beginning / to unwind" (*Sl*, 98), he recalls his brother, pretending to be a piper with a "whitewash brush for a sporran" (*SL*, 10). He then focuses on the whitewash brush itself, recalling how it "worked like magic" (*SL*, 10), before the thread of memory darkens with images of "urine" and "cattle-dung" and "dread" (*SL*, 11), as the poet recalls the pre-Christian superstitions of childhood (Vendler, 1998: 165). The following section recalls Hugh's warnings to his younger brother about mixing with "bad boys" in the college he was "bound

for" before ending on a memory of Hugh stirring "gruel" (*SL*,
11). This is followed by a sudden, sharp burst of violence,
linked verbally with the whitewash of the second section and
the gruel of the last:

> Grey matter like gruel flecked with blood
> In spatters on the whitewash. A clean spot
> Where his head had been. (*SL*, 11–12)

Here, the ordinariness of whitewash and gruel are defamil-
iarised by their association with the murdered UDA man,
killed at the Diamond. The scene is imagined as the man saw
a car pull up, "then he saw an ordinary face / For what it was
and a gun in his own face" (*SL*, 12). The poem ends with an
apostrophe to his "dear brother" who maintains the civilities
of the quotidian life by driving his tractor across that very
same Diamond, and "keeping going". He is an "antidote" to
the violence, a "salve, a defiant Cyndyllan revitalising the
gelded world of the initial poem" (McGuckian, 1999: 18).

A similar method is used in "Two Lorries" where the
driver of "Agnew's old lorry" is remembered as "sweet-
talking my mother" with his "Belfast accent", asking her to
go to a film with him in Magherafelt. Then the perspective
shifts to "a different lorry" with a payload that will "blow the
bus station to dust and ashes" (*SL*, 13). Heaney then imagines his mother waiting in that very station, and death is personified as "a dust-faced coalman" who is now refolding
"body-bags" instead of coal sacks. The fusion of bomb ashes
and coal dust makes the point of the poem: namely, that different sorts of normality co-exist.

In "The Flight Path", the interrogation of the role of art,
specifically his own art, in the face of violence becomes explicit in an interchange that is central to both the poem and
the book. It is a poem that mimics a *Bildungsroman* of the
poet's life, describing his development and physical journeys

"Manhattan", "California", and again, the stressed importance of his sojourn in Glanmore: "So to Glanmore. Glanmore. Glanmore. Glanmore. / At bay, at one, at work, at
risk and sure" (*SL*, 23). "Jet-setting" has become so familiar
that the "jumbo" jet reminds him of "a school bus", an image
which describes the learning curve he is undergoing. Even as
he describes his travels, a fusion of the Irish and the European traditions is foregrounded: "Sweeney astray in home
truths out of Horace / *Skies change, not cares, for those who
cross the sea*" (*SL*, 24).

In section four of this poem, that debate which has sim-
mered through the body of his work becomes overt, as a figure out of Heaney's "personal and political past irrupts into
the scene of the poem" (Murphy, 2000a: 93). On a "May
morning, nineteen-seventy-nine" he is confronted by "this one
I'd last met in a dream". He describes the dream where he
had been asked by this school friend, presumably a member of
the Provisional IRA, to "drive a van", presumably loaded with
explosives, "to the next customs post / At Pettigo" (*SL*, 24),
and then leave it and get driven home "in a Ford" (*SL*, 25).
Now, in a railway carriage, their encounter is more real, and
it encapsulates the antinomy that we have been tracing in his
work between the political and the aesthetic:

> "When, for fuck's sake, are you going to write
> Something for us?" "If I do write something,
> Whatever it is, I'll be writing for myself." (*SL*, 25)

This interchange has been termed "an angry 'Station Island'-
ish encounter" (Goodby and Phillips, 2001: 249), but I would
argue that it has a larger significance within Heaney's work.
This notion of the gradual prioritisation of the developing
self as against a self that is predefined by the givens of community has been at the core of Heaney's development. That
it should find such direct expression here would seem to
indicate that it is still an ongoing preoccupation. The point at

issue here is that Heaney's developing sense of selfhood can stand outside the nationalist calls for violence: he can remain a nationalist, and speak out on issues of nationalist interest, but it is on his own terms. However, this very complexity of response can cause him to criticise his own sense of balance.

In "Weighing In", he describes that delicate balance between self and community, self and other, Irishness as an essence and Irishness as part of a broader world culture. Using a "56 lb. weight" as an image, he writes of balancing this weight against another one:

> On a well adjusted, freshly greased weighbridge —
> And everything trembled, flowed with give and take. (*SL*, 17)

This is precisely that strand of imagery of balance and process that has been the focus of our inquiry. This again seems to mirror the imagery of weights used in "The Settle Bed" and poem xl from "Squarings". Also, the idea of balance is very explicit in the collection's ambiguous title, *The Spirit Level*. It explains that sense of complexity of the self that we have seen as paralleling a more complex sense of Irishness in the broader public sphere. However, those appetites of gravity still exert their own force, and part of him is angry at his own tact: "Two sides to every question, yes, yes, yes", and wishes for a more overt stance on some issues:

> Still, for Jesus' sake,
> Do me a favour would you, just this once?
> Prophesy, give scandal, cast the stone. (*SL*, 18)

So, in "The Flight Path", having asserted the rights of the individual to follow his own path, the next section talks of his translation of the "Ugolino" passage from Dante in *Field Work*, and locates the political context of this translation in terms of "its emotional entanglement in the circumstances of the 'dirty protest' begun by the internee Ciaran Nugent in Long Kesh internment camp in Northern Ireland in the late

1970s" (Corcoran, 1998: 190). He goes on to talk of Ciaran Nugent whose "red eyes" were like "something out of Dante's scurfy hell" and imagines himself, following "behind the righteous Virgil / As safe as houses and translating freely" (*SL*, 25). That duality of perspective, that slight sense of guilt about his own non-committal stance, even though it is a principled stance, surfaces here again, further complicating that sense of selfhood and individuality. It is as if, heading towards that different shore, there are eddies and tidal flows that pull him back.

In a further translation, though in this case it is a very free translation, Heaney creates a stunning drama based on Aeschylus's *Agamemnon*, the first play in the *Oresteia* trilogy, in "Mycenae Lookout". This poem examines, "through the aftermath of the Trojan War" the aftermath of "Northern Ireland's quarter-century of conflict":

> The Mycenae Lookout, Heaney's surrogate, is the Watchman in Agamemnon's palace. Conscious of the initiating sacrifice of Iphigenia by her father, privy to the adultery of Clytemnestra and Aegisthus during Agamemnon's absence at Troy, the Watchman is the helpless bystander at the murder of the returned Agamemnon, and the equally helpless witness to the prophecies of the raped Cassandra. (Vendler, 1998: 156)

This complex web of connections is further complicated when one takes into account that:

> Aegisthus is, in fact, Agamemnon's cousin, the only surviving child of Thyestes, whose other children were murdered, baked in a pie and served up to Thyestes by Agamemnon's father Atreus, in an act of revenge for Thyestes' having seduced his wife and disputed his right to reign in Argos. Clytemnestra's own rationale for killing her husband is in part driven

> by Agamemnon's having acceded to the sacrificial
> slaying of their daughter Iphigenia, during the early
> stages of the Trojan campaign. (Murphy, 2000a: 104)

The Watchman is infected by the cycle of violence: "I'd dream of blood in bright webs in a ford" (*SL*, 29). His dream indicates someone who has been desensitised by the "killing-fest", whose tongue is compared, anachronistically, to "the dropped gangplank of a cattle truck" which is "running piss and muck" (*SL*, 29). Yet in ways he is a liminal figure who is "honour-bound" to "concentrate attention out beyond / The city and the border" (*SL*, 29), and hence is both part of, and apart from, the violence. The self-description of his work as an "in-between-times that I had to row through" (*SL*, 29), and of himself as "balanced between destiny and dread" (*SL*, 30), further reinforces the correspondence between himself and Heaney, as fears and doubts about the end of the violence abound in this dark poem.

The jagged, syntactically broken, two-stress and three-stress lines which are used to describe Cassandra, in tandem with the unusually forthright language, captures the wrenching of the girl from her home and her people:

> Her soiled vest,
> Her little breasts,
> her clipped, devest-
>
> ated, scabbed
> punk head,
> the char-eyed
>
> famine gawk —
> she looked
> camp-fucked. (*SL*, 30–1)

Here the stark realities of violence, what it can do to the mind and the body, are laid out before us in bleak and crude imagery. There is little "evasion or artistic tact " (*SI*, 83) to be found in this poem. Through the different shores of the classical world, he is able to provide a devastating critique of the effects of violence on the individual. Here, the "human lot" of *Laments* is stark and violent; as he puts it: "No such thing / as innocent / bystanding" (*SL*, 30). He uses a similarly truncated line to describe Agamemnon's homecoming:

> Old King Cock-
> of-the-Walk
> was back,
>
> King Kill-
> the-Child-
> and-Take-
>
> What-Comes. (*SL*, 31–2)

Cassandra's prophecies merely encourage in the "bystanders" (and we remember that none of these are innocent) "a wish to rape her again" (Vendler, 1998: 171), as she is foretelling the future killing of Clytemnestra and Aegisthus by Orestes, the son of Clytemnestra and Agamemnon, "who will be driven from Argos by the Furies as a result of these killings" (Murphy, 2000a: 106). Cassandra's death and that of her "Troy reaver" (*SL*, 33) is described in similarly brutal terms: "to the knife / to the killer wife" (*SL*, 32). There are echoes of "Punishment" and "Kinship" in this poem, but the language is "more brutal and less equivocal" (Murphy, 2000a: 105).

The next section, "His Dawn Vision", is governed by the sonorous image: "I felt the beating of the huge time-wound / We lived inside" (*SL*, 34); while "The Nights" section outlines how the Watchman betrayed his master, Agamemnon, by hearing, but not telling, of the plans of Clytemnestra and Aegisthus. He is "much favoured" but full of "selfloathing" (*SL*, 35), and makes the point that he, like all the others, is poi-

soned by Eros and Thanatos — sex and death. "Eros–
Thanatos pairings generally do seem to rely on a perception
of woman as channel for masculine fear and desire"
(Coughlin, 1997: 196), and here we are told, of Aegisthus and
Clytemnestra, that "their real life was the bed" (*SL*, 34), while
the fall of Troy is described in terms of rape and violence:

> But in the end Troy's mothers
> bore their brunt in alley,
> bloodied cot and bed.
> The war put all men mad. (*SL*, 35–6)

Only in the last section is a different shore of hope allowed
to permeate the poem through images of "fresh water", of a
"filled bath, still unentered / and unstained" (*SL*, 36) and of
wells being sunk. As Corcoran notes, Watchman and poet
almost fuse in this image of healing water, given its preva-
lence in Heaney's writing: "The Diviner"; "Personal Heli-
con"; "Rite of Spring"; "Undine"; "Broagh"; "Anahorish";
"Sunlight"; "Grotus and Conventina"; the ending of *The Cure
at Troy*; and "at the Wellhead" (Corcoran, 1998: 202–3).
One could add the introduction to his translation of *Beowulf*
to this list, as here, water figures as an image of linguistic and
cultural complexity and fusion. In the final section of "Mycenae Lookout", the image of the ladder between the well and
the Acropolis becomes fused with:

> this ladder of our own that ran
> deep into a well-shaft being sunk
> in broad daylight, men puddling at the source
>
> through tawny mud, then coming back up
> deeper in themselves for having been there,
> like discharged soldiers testing the safe ground. (*SL*, 37)

Here we see a different shore from the rest of the landscape
of "Mycenae Lookout", as possibilities can be found even in

this grim and internecine environment. It is as if he is positing a different future from that mooted by Cassandra. Orestes will, with the intervention of the goddess Pallas Athene,
return to Argos, so perhaps Heaney is making the point that
some form of peace and hope may be possible in Ireland. His
ability to capture the optimism of a future which is forever
haunted by the imperatives of the past is one of the major
strengths of his poetry, and at the same time, one of those
nodal points at which his work intersects with the fundamental concerns of the contemporary Irish psyche. As
Goodby and Phillips have put it: "it is this doubleness in his
best poetry which explains its attractions" (Goodby and
Phillips, 2001: 246), and revisions of aspects of his earlier
work contribute to this doubleness.

We have already noted the appearance, in revised form,
of aspects of Heaney's earlier work in *The Cure at Troy*.
Goodby and Phillips trace a similar strand of revisitation of
his work through *The Spirit Level*, noting that "A Brigid's Gir-
dle" contains allusions to four of his earlier collections, while
"The Flight Path", recalling a "'Station Island'-ish encounter
with a Republican paramilitary", imports a "tercet from
Heaney's translation of the 'Ugolino' section of Dante's *Inferno*" (Goodby and Phillips, 2001: 249). This is an important
aspect of Heaney's aesthetic, and again, it stresses the developmental dimension of his work. He is constantly revising
and complicating positions which he has earlier adopted, as
he creates a fluid structure which has room for the immanent and the transcendent.

In this sense, translation as genre might well be seen as a
synecdoche of his poetic methodology, as he takes a piece of
writing, usually from the past, and from another culture, and
imbues it with resonances of his own culture. This double
perspective, with allusions and resonances feeding off each
other, suggests that the Irish experience is not merely *sui
generis*; rather is it more fully understood when juxtaposed

with European exemplars. As Catharine Malloy and Phyllis Carey have perceptively pointed out, translation has become "a paradigm of Heaney's aesthetic" (Malloy and Carey, 1996: 21). We have seen how this has been true in terms of *Sweeney Astray* and *The Cure at Troy*, and it is also an important factor in his translation of Sophocles' *Antigone*, entitled *The Burial at Thebes*. As is increasingly the case in Heaney's writing, he tends to view the matter of Ireland best through the lens of another language and culture, imitating the desire of Stephen Dedalus to fly by those nets of language, nationality and religion.

In a piece published in *The Irish Book Review*, "Thebes via Toomebridge: Retitling *Antigone*", Heaney sets out the connections between local and universal that motivated the title of this translation. Speaking of Francis Hughes, the dead hunger striker and neighbour of his in County Derry, Heaney stresses the body of Hughes as a site of struggle between the security forces and the nationalist crowd who came to take possession of it. Ownership of the body becomes a seminal metaphor here, as it becomes a potent signifier of the contest between the "instinctive powers of feeling, love and kinship" and the "daylight gods of free and self-conscious, social and political life", to quote Hegel (Heaney, 2005: 13). Heaney sees the motivation behind the "surge of rage in the crowd as they faced the police" as an index of what he terms *dúchas* (Heaney, 2005: 13), and it is here that we come to *Antigone*'s retitling. For her sense of propriety and integrity come from that feeling of kinship with the other as a fellow human, regardless of the political differences that separate us.

The scene is set after an invading army from Argos has been defeated by the Thebans under their new king Creon. Two of the sons of Oedipus, brothers to Antigone and Ismene, died in this battle: Eteocles perished defending Thebes; but his brother, Polyneices, was part of the attacking army and hence a traitor:

> Their banners flew, the battle raged
> They fell together, their father's sons. (*BT*, 8)

The Theban king, Creon, outraged by this treachery from one of the royal family, decrees that Polyneices shall not receive the normal purifying burial rites and places under interdict of death anyone who will attempt to provide these rites to the corpse. He decrees that Polyneices, that "anti-Theban Theban", will not be accorded burial but will be left to rot in the open. The results are that "The dogs and birds are at it day and night, spreading reek and rot" (*BT*, 44). Creon justifies this, in a manner similar to the British authorities and their treatment of the corpse of Francis Hughes:

> This is where I stand where it comes to Thebes
> Never to grant traitors and subversives
> Equal footing with loyal citizens
> But to honour patriots in life and death. (*BT*, 11)

For Antigone, the duty she has to her brother as human far surpasses her duty to the Theban notion of patriotism as laid down by Creon and, interestingly, she cites a higher law than that of Creon or Thebes itself:

> I disobeyed the law because the law was not
> The law of Zeus nor the law ordained
> By Justice. Justice dwelling deep
> Among the gods of the dead (*BT*, 20–1)

By positing a higher order of the treatment of the other than that of the *polis*, or group, Antigone is voicing the perennial debate between ethics and patriotism or nationalism and, more crucially in terms of Heaney's work, between the society, or tribe, and the individual.

Her stress is on the rights and duties of the individual to other individuals, or in Levinasian terms, to the face of the other. Interestingly, Creon is not depicted as some sort of political fundamentalist; he is a heroic figure in his own right who has done the state some service. He has saved Thebes from its enemies and voices a sense of patriotic philosophy which underwrites his personal ideology. His views on the *polis* and its need to impose order could well serve as a credo for many states in the world:

> For the patriot
> Personal loyalty always must give way
> To patriotic duty.
>   Solidarity, friends,
> Is what we need. The whole crew must close ranks.
> The safety of our state depends upon it. (*BT*, 10)

The stress here is on the individual as defined by his or her group. It is a sentiment similar to that of Odysseus in *The Cure at Troy*, where the choices of definition are binary: one is either Greek or Trojan. For Creon, the binary is parallel: one is either a patriot or a traitor; and this carries through in life and death.

The need to see these bodies as signifiers of patriotism or betrayal after death is a potent trope in nationalist rhetoric in an Irish as well as a classical context. The images of dead martyrs or traitors are the motive forces behind so many of the commemorative parades, processions and demonstrations that have caused such tension, bloodshed and death throughout the history of Northern Ireland. The honouring of one's own glorious dead and the dishonouring of those who broke the code of the tribe is a vital signifier in nationalist and unionist rhetorical structures. These bodies, like that of Francis Hughes, have lost all individual resonance; they have been transposed into ideological signifiers, and it is this process of ideological transformation that is being assayed by Creon as he refuses burial to Polyneices. By so doing, he attempts to attenuate the humanity of Polyneices; he is to be buried without "any ceremony whatsoever" and is adjudged to be merely a "carcass for the dogs and birds to feed on" (*BT*, 11).

From the perspective of his tribe, this punishment may well seem justified, and in his poem "Punishment", as we have seen, Heaney enunciates this tribal voice by claiming that he can "understand" the nature of such group dynamics. However, one of the strengths of Heaney's ongoing process of translation is the complication of the voice of the tribe through the sense of a permeation of self with other — the "throughotherness" that was a key factor in the transformation of Philoctetes' consciousness in *The Cure at Troy*. Similarly, in this play, it is Antigone who attempts to steer the course of humanity to a different shore. To treat the dead correctly and with honour, she implies, is very much an index of our own humanity. The treatment of people as less than human, as often demanded by the voice of the tribe, is the antithesis of her own actions. Antigone's is an evocation of a higher, inter-subjective sense of ethics:

> This proclamation had your force behind it
> But it was mortal force, and I, also a mortal,
> I chose to disregard it. I abide
> By statutes utter and immutable –
> Unwritten, original, god-given laws. (*BT*, 21)

One of the strongest points about this translation is the degree of moral complexity involved. Antigone, unlike Philoctetes, is not a particularly attractive character; she is unyielding, especially to her sister Ismene, and can be seen as almost naïve in her demand for honour for her brother. From his own perspective, and indeed, from that of the chorus, Creon is to be admired:

> Creon saved us
> Saved the country, and there he was, strong king,
> Strong head of family, the man in charge. (*BT*, 49)

However, so is Antigone, as in death she teaches Creon that, "until we breathe our last breath / we should keep the established law" (*BT*, 48). In this line we see the credo of both original and translation: our common humanity should transcend our differences. It is the treatment of the dead, themselves no longer part of politics as agents, that is seen as wrong in the dramatic logic of the play and the translation. As Heaney calls it in his prose piece, "it is a matter of burial refused", as Polyneices is being made a "non-person" (Heaney, 2005: 13) and this is what Antigone cannot countenance, and it is this disrespect for the human in death that is the cause of the metaphorical contagion outlined by the blind seer Tiresias (who has a parallel function to that of the chorus in *The Cure at Troy*):

> spreading reek and rot
> On every altar stone and temple step, and the gods
> Are revolted. That's why we have this plague,
> This vile pollution. (*BT*, 44)

The result is that the tapestry of the power structure that Creon is attempting to consolidate unravels in a litany of dead bodies: Antigone, Haemon, Eurydice all lie dead by the end of the play. The dangers of the hegemony of the *polis* as opposed to the rights of the individual are signified in the tragic conclusion of the play. Heaney, in his classical translations, has made the choice of the individual over the group an ethical trope, and this trope can be seen to derive from his Field Day pamphlet *An Open Letter*, wherein he prioritises the individual over the group for the first time.

In this poem, there is no group or proto-nationalist agenda here: "I'll stick to *I*. Forget the *we*" (*OL*, 9). He goes on to cite the example of Horace, the Roman poet who fought at the Battle of Philippi in November, 42 BC which ended with the rout of Brutus's army and the suicides of both Brutus and Cassius. Heaney's reference to Horace who "threw away his shield to be / A naked I" (*OL*, 9) as "exemplary," speaks volumes for his notion of the role of the poet in such a political situation. To see Heaney as voicing the victimhood of Ireland in this poem is to remain totally locked within a Manichean notion of a simplified colonial/ postcolonial epistemology. His broadness of contextual allusion, his purposeful inclusion of Livy's cry of each man for himself, and his citing of Horace's exemplary act of throwing away his shield so as to become a "naked I", should convince us that this poem is meant to end the "simple history lesson" and instead, to begin a new one wherein the subject, located within a broad contextual frame of reference is, almost by definition, plural, open and definitely complex, as opposed to singular and single-minded.

Antigone is similarly focused on the need to value an individual *qua* individual, as opposed to an ideological member of a group. For her, there is a higher bond than mere tribal patriotism. This is evident in her words to Creon, where she speaks of "Justice dwelling deep / Among the gods of the dead" and "Unwritten, original, god-given laws" (*BT*, 21). It is this sense of a law higher than that of tribal politics that unites Antigone with Philoctetes; they both feel that there is a higher court of appeal and for Heaney, this gestures towards both that sense of the throughother, and that ideal of the further shore that inform his ethical aesthetic. Just as the chorus in *The Cure at Troy* are the voice of reality and justice, so Antigone also sees herself as a servant of justice; "Justice won't allow it" (*BT*, 25). This justice transcends the immanent calls of the tribe and instead looks towards the further shore of an intersubjective sense of the value of each human life. In this sense, Heaney's work is ethical to its core. How-

ever, to see these translations as locked in the symbolic order of the ancient classical world is to miss the subtext that
is at work here. In this text, as in *The Cure at Troy*, there is
an almost allegorical level of connection between classical
Greece and contemporary Northern Ireland. The image of a
woman pleading, and then demanding, justice for a dead
brother had a particular resonance in Ireland in 2005.

The body of Francis Hughes, and the body of Polyneices
are answered, in the contemporary moment, by the body of
Robert McCartney, someone who was killed within his *polis*,
but who, metaphorically, is a revenant, unable to rest. On 30
January 2005, Robert McCartney was murdered outside Ma-
gennis's pub in the Short Strand area of Belfast. Reputedly,
the murderers were members of Sinn Féin and the Provisional IRA, and in the aftermath of the murder, the pub was
cleaned of fingerprints, CCTV evidence was removed and
threats were issued to the witnesses of the act as to the
consequences of reporting any of this to the Police Service
of Northern Ireland.

The sisters of Robert McCartney — Catherine, Paula,
Claire, Donna and Gemma — and his partner Bridgeen, have
spoken out in a campaign to see justice done for their
brother in death, and this is eerily resonant of the voice of
Antigone in defence of her own dead brother. Their demand
is for justice to be done for their brother, a demand that
echoes across the centuries, and that could be spoken in the
words of Antigone. It is significant that Heaney, in describing
the genesis of this text, compares the treatment of the body
of Polyneices with that of Francis Hughes, the hunger-
striker; it is even more significant that this play deals with
the voice of women — then, as now, seen as not quite part
of the public sphere — women who are totally focused on
obtaining justice for the dead:

> I never did a nobler thing than bury
> My brother Polyneices. And if these men
> Weren't so afraid to sound unpatriotic
> They'd say the same. (*BT*, 23)

The partner and sisters of Robert McCartney have suffered the same fate as that of Antigone; they are seen as unusual voices in the public sphere: "women were never meant for this assembly" (*BT*, 27), says Creon, words that have a chilling echo in the warning for the sisters by Martin McGuiness about being used by other political forces. Here, the ethical has engaged with the political, and the political is found wanting in the face of that imperative towards justice that has become symbolised by the name and body of Robert McCartney.

The women who spoke out for their brothers, both in classical drama and in the contemporary world of the political, are ethical voices who demand justice, and common human decency that goes beyond narrow loyalty to the *polis*, the tribe or any ideology that seeks to dehumanise those who are on the other side. The following lines have a double resonance, both within the text and the current political, as they state the role of women in the public sphere:

> Two women on our own
> Faced with a death decree –
> Women, defying Creon?
> It's not a woman's place.
> We're weak where they are strong. (*BT*, 5)

This public sphere which is deemed to be not a woman's place is both ancient Thebes and contemporary Belfast. One can do no better then wish that those who killed him can take the advice of Tiresias, the blind prophet:

Yield to the dead. Don't stab a ghost.
What can you win when you only wound a corpse?
(44)

These words, uttered in the present context, attest the lasting value of this translation by Seamus Heaney of Sophocles'
Antigone. This venerable text still speaks to us across the
centuries, and the language of this translation, lucid, crisp
and intelligent, makes that voice seem ever more relevant.

Interestingly, given that Heaney has been accused by
some feminist critics of not being sufficiently open to em-
powering tropes of women, his portrayal of Antigone would
seem to give the lie to this criticism. While in his bog poems, the point can be made, and has been made, most force-
fully by Pat Coughlin, that he surrenders to traditional imagery of woman as passive receptor of male action, Antigone's strong line of action and discourse would seem to
contradict this perspective. In a culture where women had
little value, she defies the law, the state and the king and ultimately triumphs by proving her point and obtaining proper
burial for her brother. Again, the strength of this text is the
focus on the individual. Creon is far from the two-
dimensional figure of evil with whom we have become familiar over recent years as complex political issues are attenu-
ated into a just war against "bad guys" whose names have
been almost domesticated for familiarity: Saddam, bin Laden,
Arafat.

At the end of the play, as Creon ponders the wreckage
of his personal and political life, he utters the poignant
phrase: "I have wived and fathered death" (*BT*, 54).

Here, translation from the classical Greek culture provides both distance and an exemplary text which allows for
commentary on the contemporary situation while at the
same time offering sufficient ethical and aesthetic distance.
For Heaney, this has been the ongoing value of translation.

This same sense of the imaginative power of translation as an aesthetic vehicle is also a factor in two of his other translations: *Laments*, by Jan Kochanowski; and *The Midnight Verdict*, a translation of part of Brian Merriman's poem, placed in a framework of two translated sections from Ovid's *Metamorphoses*.

Laments voices the personal sense of loss felt by the sixteenth-century Polish poet Jan Kochanowski at the death of his daughter Orszula. In it, Heaney probes issues of loss, despair, regret, and the sheer sense of hopelessness that can be brought about by the death of a loved one. There has been relatively little written about this translation within Heaney criticism, especially compared to the attention given to his *Beowulf* translation. If we ask ourselves what attracted Heaney to this collaboration with Stanisław Barańczak, who teaches Polish literature at Harvard, we come up with some interesting answers.

In a literate introduction, Barańczak notes that this poem was written by a man who was a "Renaissance poet *par excellence*" (*L*, vii). Kochanowski's learning is clear from the translation, and names from classical Greece and Rome abound in this poem: Heraclitus, Simonides, Pluto, Persephone, Charon, Sappho, Brutus and a sustained allusion to the Orpheus myth. Given the strain of similar allusiveness in Heaney's own work, a sense of kindred enterprise with a poet who was attempting to broaden the horizons of a language and a literature can be detected. Barańczak points out that the poem has been read as coming into conflict with contemporary social and literary custom, namely the "classical principle of *decorum*" which reserved the genre of lament or threnody for "heroes, military leaders, statesmen, great thinkers" (*L*, xv). Consequently the initial reaction to the original poem was unfavourable. Alternatively, the poem, with the benefit of a post-Romantic sensibility, has been read as a "logbook of personal suffering", as the work of a poet who "rejects rigid rules in favour of unrestricted spontaneity of expression" (*L*, xvi).

Interestingly, Barańczak himself espouses neither view. He suggests that a more correct reading would be to see the dramatic power of *Laments* as being born from:

> the clash of the rebellion and the rule, the latter still a factor commanding enough to have to be reckoned with . . . Just as in *Laments*, expressions of religious doubt that border on blasphemy can be pronounced because their speaker still thinks, argues, levels his accusations or asks his questions in the symbolic language of religion, so the breaking of the Classical rules gives the poetry positively new force and import because the rules are still recognized as an abiding presence. (*L*, xvi)

In other words, it is the structure of dialectic, of process, of a poetic which encompasses different elements which reflect and refract each other that makes this poem what it is. The parallels with the Heaney we have been discussing are clear. The poem dramatises that trope of crossing which has been so important to Heaney, as Kochanowski moves from shore to shore, emotionally and culturally, with the process being the most absorbing factor.

Thus, Heaney can focus on the moments of rebellion in the poem, as the poet rails against the injustice of his daughter's "Ungodly Death" (*L*, 9); "she'd asked the good God to ward off / Everything bad" (*L*, 25); "That the Lord's hand could destroy / In one stroke all my joy"; "His blow shattered my bliss" (*L*, 39). However, he can also trace a contrary movement as the poet, realising that reason can in no way console him, turns to the transcendent: "God is my only hope" (*L*, 41).

And in the final sections of the poem, this movement becomes stronger "My Lord, each of us is your wilful child";

"Have pity, Lord, on my despair and pain" (*L*, 43); "The Lord's ways are not ours. / Our task is simply to accord with them" (*L*, 51) and finally "You must accept although your wound's still raw" (*L*, 53). It is the ability to contain both strands and to set up an interaction between them that makes the poem interesting.

In no way does this conclusion diminish the grief or anger of the earlier parts of the poem: instead, it demonstrates the ability, indeed, the necessity, for human consciousness to be able to encompass more than one position. The final resolution comes in a dream vision: "I saw my mother, holding in her arms / My Ursula" (*L*, 45). Interestingly, his mother says that it is his cries that have disturbed "my distant shore" (*L*, 45). She goes on to provide that spectral advice that has been such a familiar Heaney trope throughout his work, and it is advice that, given the vastly different contexts, has similarities with that of some of the shades from *Station Island*:

> Weigh up your losses, ponder each mistake,
> Yet never overlook what is at stake:
> Your peace of mind, your equanimity! . . .
> Be your own master. (*L*, 51)

The value of learning, of the very erudition which connects Kochanowski, Barańczak and Heaney himself, and which has been of benefit to others, is called on in a manner redolent of "Exposure" and some of the questioning poems of *Field Work*: "By now your grafting should have yielded fruit . . . Now, master, you will have to heal yourself" (*L*, 53). This "grafting" is another name for that process which we have seen as central to Heaney's work and, by extension, to the ongoing exfoliation of notions of Irishness (as well as linking to the idea of "hard graft" or hard work). The grafting of aspects of alterity onto those of the self is precisely how societal and cultural change comes about, both at the per-

sonal and the communal level. The fruit of such graftings is
the Irelands of the mind of which we have been speaking.

   This question of the role of the aesthetic in the face of
suffering is one which has long been of concern in Heaney's
work. That he should find common ground with Kochanowski should hardly surprise us, especially given the similarity in
their use of hauntings from the other shore to demonstrate
the need for otherness in any conception of identity. One
thinks of the interrogative "What is my apology for poetry?"
(*FW*, 41) from Sonnet IX of the "Glanmore Sonnets", and
the similarity is again clear. The questioning of the value of
art, reason and religion in the face of suffering and loss is a
further connective tissue between the original and the translation. Heaney manages to inject enough of his own tone
into the work to set off those resonances with alterity that
have been a central concern.

   The conclusion of the poem demonstrates similar affinities with Heaney's own process of questioning:

<blockquote>
The wax
And wane of things, and nothing more; the flux
Of new events, now painful, now serene;
He who has grasped this accepts what has been
And what will be with equal steadfastness,
Resigned to suffer, glad to suffer less.
Bear humanly the human lot. (*L*, 53)
</blockquote>

The close of the poem, asking the poet to "bear humanly the
human lot" encapsulates much of Heaney's own process of
questioning, as he attempts to explore and expand the nature
of his own individual humanity as opposed to a predefined
group identity. We have come a long way from the understanding of the "exact / and tribal, intimate revenge" (*N*, 38),
and from the notion of slaughter for the common good. This
sense of commonality has been superseded by one of individuality, and it is the individuality of Kochanowski, that hu-

man spark which caused him to defy poetic and cultural convention and avail of an elevated poetic form to enunciate a
very personal grief that, I would maintain, connects him intel-
lectually and emotionally with Heaney.

It is the "flux of new events" that should be the focus of
the poet. These may be either happy or sad, but if they are
faced with humanity, then the work of the poet is being
done. This quest for humanity in the face of adversity is a
strong connecting bond, and the trans-cultural symphysis
demonstrates the value of translation. Grief, to change texts
for a moment, is neither Greek nor Trojan alone, nor is it
Irish or English, nationalist or unionist. It exists across the
spread of the human family, a point that Heaney's use of
other languages and cultures has already reinforced, but
which has a new actuality when we look at the suffering and
pain caused by the death of a "thirty-month-old child" (*L*,
25). The levels of insight into the complexity of the human
psyche that Heaney has provided are matched by the seventh lament, where the poet can hardly look at the clothes
worn by his daughter. He tells us that they are "pathetic gar-
ments" because they "miss her body's warmth; and so do I"
(*L*, 15). Like Orpheus or Dante, the poet too would "enter
the dark realm below" and use his lovely lute "before stern
Pluto, soften him / With songs and tears" until he relents
and "lets my dear girl go" (*L*, 29). This, while recalling "The
Crossing", with which we began this section, and the
underworld poems in which his father figured from *Seeing
Things*, also leads us into the next translation which Heaney
undertook.

The Midnight Verdict is a *locus classicus* of the trend in
Heaney's poetry which we have been following as his work
has developed. He gives us an account of its genesis in the
introduction, and it serves as an index of the broad sweep of
his imagination, as well as indicating how he always attempts
to place an Irish text within a broader, classical context. The

poetic depth charge is to be found in the interaction of the two. He tells us that the "three translations here were all part of a single impulse". He had translated the "Orpheus and Eurydice" lines in 1993, and then, on being asked to lecture at the Merriman Summer School on *Cúirt an Mheán-Oíche*, he began "to put bits of the Irish into couplets":

> and, in doing so, gradually came to think of the Merriman poem in relation to the story of Orpheus, and in particular the story of his death as related by Ovid. The end of *The Midnight Court* took on a new resonance when read within the acoustic of the classical myth. (*MV*, 11)

The Midnight Court deals with the dream vision of the poet, Brian Merriman, who is accused, as a representative of Irish manhood, by the women of Ireland:

> At the Midnight Court, which is ruled entirely by women, Aoibheall [the fairy queen of Munster] outlines the problem: men are reluctant to marry, the population is falling, and the fairy host has mandated her to set up a court in place of the English ones, and to propose a solution. (Kiberd, 2000: 187)

The poem features an anguished debate between a young woman and an old man. She is angry at being sexually neglected — "I'm scorched and tossed, a sorry case / Of nerves and drives and neediness" — who goes on to describe herself as a "throbbing ache" and a "numb discord" (*MV*, 29), with her final solution to the problem being expressed in the couplet: "For if things go on like this, then fuck it! / The men will have to be abducted!" (*MV*, 29).

After this speech, in a section not translated in *The Midnight Verdict*, the old man explains how he was tricked into marrying a young woman who was already pregnant. The young woman responds in kind, asking why the clergy cannot marry, and all wait for Aoibheall's verdict, which is delivered at the end of the poem, with the figure of Merriman serving as synecdoche for the men of Ireland:

> But it's you and your spunkless generation.
> You're a source blocked off that won't refill.
> You have failed your women, one and all. (*MV*, 26)

The poet, as representative of men, comes under particular attack, as an average "Passable male — no paragon / But nothing a woman wouldn't take on". He is seen as spending his life on pleasure, "Playing his tunes, on sprees and batters / With his intellectual and social betters" (*MV*, 32).

Heaney's notion of the importance of this poem can be gleaned from an essay in *The Redress of Poetry* entitled, revealingly, "Orpheus in Ireland: On Brian Merriman's *The Midnight Court*", wherein he outlines the value of this poem as "part of the Irish past" and of the "literary conventions of medieval Europe" while at the same time noting that it is capable of being read as "a tremor of the future" (*RP*, 39). He also notes that the poem's original audience would have seen it as a parody of the traditional *aisling* poetic form (a form in which the poet sees a beautiful woman in a dream, who "drives him to diction and description", and who is an allegory of Ireland. She generally tells of her ill-treatment by the English before consoling "herself and the poet by prophesying that her release will be affected by a young prince from overseas"). For Heaney, the poem is, among other things, "a blast of surrealistic ridicule directed against such a fantasy" (*RP*, 48), and given his own far less overt attempts at prising open nationalist tropes and images, we can see how this dimension of the poem would be attractive to him. It is a way of gesturing towards that different shore by using farce and surrealism:

> *Cúirt an Mhéan-Oíche* was important because it spon-
> sored a libertarian and adversarial stance against the
> repressive conditions which prevailed during those
> years in Irish life, public and private. (*RP*, 53)

The role of the poet in this court of appeal is also central.
Merriman himself figures in the poem as a narrative voice
and witness to the debate, though near the end of the poem,
he becomes the scapegoat for the crimes of the men of Ireland. He figures as the artist, "Playing his tunes" (*MV*, 32),
and is called by his "nickname 'merry man' ", as well as being
seen as "the virgin merry, going grey", and finally being referred to as "Mr Brian" (*MV*, 33). The deprecating tone is
reminiscent of many of Heaney's own comments about his
early self: "I hate how quick I was to know my place" (*SI*,
85); or "while I sit here with a pestering / Drouth for
words" (*N*, 59). However, the learning in the poem makes it
clear that Merriman too was attempting to redefine an Irish
poetic trope within a broader cultural context:

> Merriman wrote in rhyming couplets, which varied
> the rhyme from couplet to couplet in a manner
> never attempted by his predecessors in Irish. This
> fact alone has led admirers to suggest the influence
> of Goldsmith, Swift and Pope, . . . Merriman infused
> older Gaelic forms with the techniques of Augustan
> writing. (Kiberd, 2000: 184)

It is this broader aspect of the poem, parodying Irish traditional genres, while experimenting with innovative rhyme
schemes in the Irish language by looking outwards towards
the English poetic tradition, that interests Heaney, and that
brought this remarkable edition of this translation into being.

Heaney tells us that, as he translated these lines from
Merriman, he began to see elements of Ovid's *Metamorphoses* reflected in them, specifically the story of Orpheus

and Eurydice. He goes on to quote from the conclusion of the opening part of Book X, telling how, after Eurydice had "died again", Orpheus was "Disconsolate, beyond himself, dumbfounded" and the result was a transformation: "and Orpheus / Withdrew and turned away from loving women" (*MV*, 18). The only bride for Orpheus would now be "a boy" and Heaney detected a distant parallel between:

> the situation of this classical poet figure, desired by those he has spurned, and the eighteenth-century Irish poet as he appears at the end of *Cúirt an Mhéan-Oíche*, arraigned for still being a virgin when the country is full of women who'd be only too glad to ease him of his virtue. (*RP*, 58)

Both texts place the artist in some form of trial, and here we are on the familiar ground of Heaney's own constant interrogations about whether his role is to be one of the brothers bound in a ring (*FW*, 22), or else to be somewhere "well out, beyond" (*FW*, 24), attempting to "fill the element / with signatures on your own frequency" (*SI*, 93–4).

The Irish poem, Heaney maintains, can be read as another manifestation of the story of Orpheus, "master poet of the lyre, the patron, and sponsor of music and song" (*RP*, 58), and the different conclusions of both poems depict the different cultures involved. Orpheus, singing in the woods, is spied by a band of "crazed Ciconian women" who call him "Orpheus the misogynist" and attack him: the "furies were unleashed" (*MV*, 39), and they turned to "rend the bard" (*MV*, 40). The Irish parallel has a tamer ending. As the women decide to "Flay him alive" and to "Cut deep. No mercy. Make him squeal / Leave him in strips from head to heel" (*MV*, 33), the poet wakes up: "Then my dreaming ceased / And I started up, awake, released" (*MV*, 34). Heaney tends to read one ending in the light of the other, yet another of those transformative crossings of self and other, as Ovid is read through Merriman and Merriman through Ovid.

The resulting structure is a triptych which features Ovid's account of the death of Eurydice and Orpheus's subsequent descent into the underworld, followed by two sections of the Merriman piece, and culminating in the death of Orpheus. Perhaps more than any other, this translation enacts the imperative towards viewing Ireland within a classical and European perspective. The three sections are all in English, but spring from two very different source languages. The very act of reading this piece is to submerge oneself in the cultural hybridity that has become contemporary Ireland, as the Irish, Greek and English languages interact and intersect in a structure which is sufficiently fluid to accommodate them all. All three poems deal with some form of transformation, so they are keenly connected with the other concerns of his translations, and the creative juxtaposition within this triptych, I would argue, has a lot to do with Heaney's assertion that *The Midnight Court* has a "role to play in the construction of a desirable civilization" (*RP*, 57).

Thus, the familiar myth of Orpheus descending to the underworld to sing, play and use his art to attempt to recover Eurydice, is connected with Kochanowski's attempts to use his art to in some way enunciate or palliate his grief, a further crossing being the latter's own use of the Orpheus myth. There is a similarity between both poems in that they feel that death has been untimely: "The snake she stepped on / Poisoned her and cut her off too soon" (*MV*, 16), recalls the lament of the father "Oh, you fell silent much too soon" (*L*, 13). The role of the victim is also foregrounded in both, recalling the focus on two different kinds of victims, Philoctetes and Neoptolemus, in *The Cure at Troy*. The comic aspect of Merriman's poem — the accusation levelled at the poet that he is an example of a whole class of Irishmen who are refusing to marry — and the anger of the unmarried women at this insult, can be read as a parody of the anger of the maenads in *Metamorphoses*.

Both poems also feature intersections between humanity and humanity's "other" — the other world, the land of death, the fairy kingdom. In both, humanity is seen struggling with what is both the non-human — fairies and death — and, paradoxically, with what can be seen as almost the defining factors of humanity, namely the aesthetic and narrative imperatives: stories of beings created out of human imagination, and stories which make death part of the human narrative through anthropomorphisation and personification of death in terms of Pluto and Charon.

In terms of the value of translation within his poetic development, a final image from *The Cure at Troy* will underline the point. Writing of entrenched communities, be they Greek and Trojan or unionist and nationalist, he notes that they are:

> People so deep into
> Their own self-pity self-pity buoys them up.
> People so staunch and true, they're fixated,
> Shining with self-regard like polished stones. (*CT*, 1)

In *The Haw Lantern*, he writes of a diametrically opposite image of stone in "The Stone Grinder", where stone is seen as grinding away present images so as to prepare for new messages and signifiers: "I ground the same stones for fifty years / and what I undid was never the thing I had done" (*HL*, 8). Instead of the presence and fixation of the "polished stones", here it is the process of grinding stones in order to prepare for the new that is valued: "For them it was a new start and a clean slate / every time" (*HL*, 8). Translation allows him to wipe the slate of fixation clean, and to dislocate and re-vision Irishness through the crossing over (an etymologically valid meaning of translation), into other cultures and languages.

This valuing of process is very much in keeping with the trend we have been examining in his translations. In the next chapter, we will use his own rationale of the process of translation in a review of Ó Tuama's and Kinsella's *Poems of the Dispossessed* in *The Government of the Tongue*, as a point of embarkation into a discussion of his prose, a neglected genre in Heaney studies. It is a genre wherein the desire to create an imagined Ireland, to reach towards that other shore which can provide a different perspective on the past, and perhaps inform the future, is further developed. His writing entails such a "responsibility toward the *future*, since it involves the struggle to create openings within which the other can appear" and can hence "come to transform what we know or think we know" (Derrida, 1992: 5) [*italics original*]. Far from being collections of literary criticism, "what emerges in these essays is a sophisticated approach to poetry" in the setting out of a carefully constructed and developing "theorization of poetry" (O'Brien, 1999b: 51).

Chapter Five

A Newer Understanding

In his review of *An Duanaire: Poems of the Dispossessed*, Heaney focuses on the value of the translation process that is overtly at work as one reads this book. These poems, collected by Professor Seán Ó Tuama, and translated by Thomas Kinsella, comprise the poetry that was written in the Irish language from 1600 to 1900, a time when that language was in a spiral of decline due to a combination of the education policies of the British government, keen to homogenise the Irish as English-speaking, and a parallel economic pressure from parents in the 1800s who, seeing emigration as the only logical course in a famine-riven culture, felt that their children would have an advantage disembarking from emigrant ships in Boston or New York if they were English-speaking. The cultural loss involved in this process was huge, as much of the literature being written in Irish was losing its audience as it was being composed.

Ó Tuama and Kinsella have provided parallel texts, with the Irish poem on one page and the English translation on the other. Heaney sees this process as attempting to heal "the hidden fault in that very phrase 'Irish poetry', by closing the rift between the Irish language past and the English language present" (*GT*, 30), and here we immediately see a connection with his own work. Issues of language and identity have long been to the fore in the politics of Ireland and Britain in general, and specifically in the politics of Northern Ireland, where these issues have become over-determined. Heaney is not interested in valorising other traditions, or in apportioning any form of historical blame. Instead, he looks for a structure capable of containing both traditions, a balance that is imagined in terms of that very sense of process and journey between different points that has been a constant thread running through his poetry.

As he puts it, reading this book is an instance of that very process of movement that he finds so valuable:

> the translations here are not asking to be taken as alternatives to the originals but are offered as paths to lead our eyes left across the page, back to the Irish. There is an ideal of service behind it all, a literary ideal, it should be stressed, not a propagandist one: we are led to the Irish poems not in order to warm ourselves at the racial embers but to encounter works of art that belong to world literature. (*GT*, 31)

This sense of seeing Irish writing, in whatever language, as part of a world literature is, of course, very much what we have seen his poetry enunciating, and much of his prose pursues the same agenda. Just as *Field Work* and *Station Island* stress the value of Dante, so Heaney's prose expands on that value. In "Envies and Identifications", Heaney stresses that Dante embodied that very balance of which he so often speaks. Osip Mandelstam, he notes, found Dante an exemplar who "wears no official badge, enforces no party line". For him, Dante "is not perceived as the mouthpiece of an orthodoxy but rather as the apotheosis of free, natural, biological processes" (*EI*, 18). Heaney goes on to imagine Ó Tuama linking the Irish poet Aodhagán Ó Rathaille with Dante (*GT*, 31) and to praise Kinsella for his long project of widening "the lens" and of making "Irish poetry in English get out from under the twilight shades of the specifically English tradition" (GT, 32).

In the following essay, Heaney goes on to expound on "The Impact of Translation" in broadly similar terms. It is a vehicle for reviving and renewing a tradition and a culture, and for allowing literature to take a lead in opening itself up to other languages, traditions and identities. This essay makes the point that it is only through translation that the Irish and English traditions can become open to the bracing effect of the poetry of Eastern Europe. He speaks of a translation of a poem by Czeslaw Miłosz, translated by Robert Pinsky, entitled "Incantation", a poem full of optimism as to the value of art in society. The poem states that "Human reason is beautiful and invincible"; it goes on to add that "It puts what should be above things as they are" (GT, 36). However, the real value of this poetic incantation is that it is "a spell, uttered to bring about a desirable state of affairs, rather than a declaration that such a state of affairs truly exists" (GT, 37). Heaney makes the point that our knowledge of Miłosz's own past reinforces this, notably, his resistance to the Nazis and his breaking of ranks with the People's Republic, which led to a lifetime of "exile and self-scrutiny" (GT, 38). The parallels with Heaney's own writing are clear here, especially in that term "self-scrutiny". Indeed, in a recent translation of a poem by Miłosz, Heaney makes this point emblematically. He calls this translation The Door Stands Open, and it is an obvious intertextual allusion to the title of his own second volume Door into the Dark. One might suggest that one of the values of translation is to allow the darkness of an inward-looking culture to be opened to the light of different perspectives; in other words, to valorise the rapport between self and other.

For Heaney, as we have seen, translations from all cultures provide a broader symbolic order through which the signifiers of a culture can be understood, and this is not just culture-specific to an Irish context. In the aftermath of September 11th, Heaney, like so many people in the western world, struggled to find images and symbols adequate to the shock of seeing the technological power of contemporary capital, embodied in towering skyscrapers, reduced to rubble. In his poem and lecture *Anything Can Happen*, Heaney again made use of translation to provide a sense of cultural context through which we can come to some form of comprehension of these cataclysmic events. Contemporary Lacanian psychoanalytic theory would suggest that language is never adequate in terms of expressing the real, and the attempts to explain and understand September 11th exemplify this.

Heaney, in his lecture accompanying this poem, touches on the same point. Asking the rhetorical question about "how exactly art earns its keep in a violent time", he provides the following answer:

> One thing is certain. The indispensable poem always has an element of surprise about it. Even perhaps a touch of the irrational. For both the reader and the writer, it will possess a soothsaying force, as if it were an oracle delivered unexpectedly and irresistibly. It will arrive like a gift from the muse, or if you prefer, the unconscious. (*AH*, 13)

Translation from a different culture can help to provide this fresh and surprising perspective. As he says in the aftermath of September 11th, there was a cry for poems that would be "equal to the moment" (*AH*, 14). This is redolent of an earlier comment in his career when, at the beginning of the violence in Northern Ireland, Heaney saw his function as providing "befitting images of adversity". And, just as we saw him look at other cultures and languages for these images, so here he recalls a poem by Horace about Jupiter the Thunder God who struck suddenly and amazed the poet. As

Heaney tells us, it is a poem about "*terra tremens*, the opposite of *terra firma*" (*AH*, 15), and he goes on:

> It was written a little over two thousand years ago
> by the Roman poet Horace, but it could have been
> written in Baghdad. In it Horace expresses the shock
> he felt when Jupiter, the thunder-god, drove his
> chariot across a clear blue sky. (*AH*, 15)

The point of the poem is the sudden nature of change — how the high can be brought low with stunning rapidity. In Horace's poem, there were no storm clouds or any warning — just that sudden irruption of power and destruction indicative of the fragility of human power and surety. For Heaney, these lines are adequate to the feelings of terror and awe that sent shock waves around the world on September 11th. For Heaney, the correspondence between the thunder of Jupiter and the thunder caused by the bombs that destroyed the Twin Towers of the World Trade Centre centres on the lines of the original poem "for the god has power to change the highest things to / for the lowest" (*AH*, 18). In his own translation or version of the poem, Heaney makes the connection all the more strong as he renders the lines as follows. The redolence of images of the fall of the Twin Towers in the third millennium necessarily colour our reading of these lines written at the beginning of the first millennium:

> Anything can happen, the tallest things
> Be overturned, those in high places daunted,
> Those overlooked regarded . . .
>
> Ground gives. The heaven's weight
> Lifts up off Atlas like a kettle lid.
> Capstones shift, nothing resettles right.
> Telluric ash and fire-spore boil away. (*AH*, 20)

And in a sense which echoes his other classical translations, it is the voice of the single individual that is the resonating device of the poem: it is "the voice of an individual in shock at what can happen to the world, so that the phrase 'anything can happen' . . . expresses the sudden casual desolation" (*AH*, 19) that accompanied the third millennium. In a manner redolent of Philoctetes and Antigone, it is the individual, as opposed to the group, that is ever the focal point of Heaney's attention.

In terms of the politics of translation, one of the most original aspects of *Anything Can Happen* is that it is published by Amnesty International but also that it is published in a volume that also features multiple translations of Heaney's version of the Horace poem, and it is a version to which he adds a new stanza of his own, and makes significant changes to the original, into Irish, Xhosa, Afrikaans, Basha Indonesian, Dutch, Hebrew, Arabic, Serbian, Bosnian, German, Russian, Chinese, Tibetan, Japanese, Malay, French, Swahili, Spanish, Basque, Hindi, Urdu, Turkish and Greek.

Interestingly, at a further level, these translations are placed across the page from languages which have traditionally been signifiers of enmity and warfare between different groups, tribes or nations. So Xhosa and Afrikaans share a single page opening, as do German and Russian, Bosnian and Serbian, etc. The effect of this is to demonstrate how languages, which are so often signifiers of difference and antagonism, can also be seen as signifiers of inclusion. The act of reading this translation of a translation, which itself is a version and a new work, sets up new relationships between the different languages. Thus the effect of the politics of translation is heightened: languages set side by side demonstrate the common humanity that connects as well as divides people. Just as the conflict between ethics and politics troubled Philoctetes in *The Cure at Troy*, and just as the parallel conflict between the law of the tribe and a greater, intersubjective sense of law drove Antigone's struggle in *The Burial at Thebes*, so similar struggles are the driving force in the writing of Heaney, and other important figures in contemporary thought, such as Derrida and Levinas.

Translation provides a broader framework from which to view the Irish experience. In the works of Eastern European writers, Heaney is able to find yet more exemplars who demonstrate that the Northern Irish situation is not unique; rather it is part of a world-wide struggle. They also demonstrate the role of the aesthetic in that struggle. Later in "The Impact of Translation", Heaney recalls the Joycean notion that "inspection of the country from the outside was the surest way of getting to the core of Irish experience" (*GT*, 40).

He goes on to modernise this dictum by suggesting that, nowadays, "the shortest way to Whitby, the monastery where Caedmon sang the first Anglo-Saxon verses, is via Warsaw and Prague" (*GT*, 41). Translation as a crossing over, as a transformative journey between cultures, has an important role in his work, and in his translation of *Beowulf*, and particularly in the long introduction which precedes it, we find this same process at work, and further explored.

This work, probably the first canonical text of the English literary tradition, begins with the exclamation "*Hwæt*". Traditionally, this has been translated as "lo", "hark", "behold", "attend" or "listen". Heaney, however, has translated it as "So" (*B*, xxvii). His explanation for so doing underlines yet again the transformative process that drives his own particular mode of translation, as self and other, Irish and English, colonised and coloniser interfuse and transform each other's discourse. Each has the ability to reach out to that different shore, and in the process become, to some degree, "allthroughother".

In the introduction, he speaks of the difficulty of finding, not the lexical meaning of the Anglo-Saxon words, but the "tuning fork that will give you the note and pitch for the overall music of the work" (*B*, xxvi). As he puts it, when speaking about the practice of translating this poem, he came to consider *Beowulf* to be part of his "voice-right" (*B*, xxiii), though such a conclusion was not easily reached. He had been asked to translate the poem by Norton in the mid 1980s, but felt that the "attempt to turn it into modern English seemed to me like trying to bring down a megalith with a toy hammer" (*B*, xxii). However, he tells us of a gradual sense of at-homeness in the Anglo-Saxon idiom, realising that the first lines of "Digging" conformed "to the requirements of Anglo-Saxon metrics", as each line was composed of "two balancing halves, each half containing two stressed syllables". This was an unconscious process but on reflection, he could say that part of him "had been writing Anglo-Saxon from the start" (*B*, xxiii).

He goes on to trace his connection with Anglo-Saxon through his Gaelic-Irish tradition, noting how words like "*lachtar*", an Irish language word which had survived in the contemporary English of his home, and "*thole*", which was a dialect word for "suffer" in County Derry, but which ultimately derived from the Anglo-Saxon "*þolian*", made him aware of the complexity of linguistic etymology:

> I tended to conceive of English and Irish as adversarial tongues, as either/or conditions rather than both/ and, and this was an attitude that for a long time hampered the development of a more confident and creative way of dealing with the whole vexed question — the question, that is, of the relationship between nationality, language, history and literary tradition in Ireland. (*B*, xxiv)

Lectures on the history of the English language in Queen's University by Professor John Braidwood made this all the more complex by pointing out that the word "whiskey" is the same word as the Irish and Scots Gaelic word "*uisce*", meaning water. Heaney found this an important connection, as the River Usk might now be seen as: "the River Uisce (or whiskey). He went on to see this image as a liberating one as "the stream was suddenly turned into a kind of linguistic river of rivers", what he terms a "riverrun of Finnegans Wakespeak" (*B*, xxiv).

This linguistic cross-fertilisation, a translation in another sense of the word, was instrumental in creating an intellectual structure which would grant the balance and complexity of which we have been speaking:

> The Irish/English duality, the Celtic/Saxon antithesis were momentarily collapsed and in the resulting etymological eddy a gleam of recognition flashed through the synapses and I glimpsed an elsewhere of potential that seems at the same time to be a somewhere remembered. The place on the language map where the Usk and the *uisce* and the whiskey coincided was definitely a place where the spirit might find a loophole, an escape route from what John Montague has called "the partitioned intellect", away into some unpartitioned linguistic country, a region where one's language would not be simply a badge of ethnicity or a matter of cultural preference or an official imposition, but an entry into further language. (*B*, xxiv–xxv)

It is with this "further language" in mind that he begins with that resonant "So", a word derived, from "a familiar local voice", one that had belonged to relatives of Heaney's father, called Scullions (*B*, xxvi). As he looked for a suitable word to translate "*hwaet*", their "Hiberno-English Scullionspeak" provided the option:

> the particle "so" came naturally to the rescue, because in that idiom "so" operates as an expression

that obliterates all previous discourse and narrative,
and at the same time functions as an exclamation
calling for immediate attention. So "so" it was. (*B*,
xxvii)

It embodies that increasing complexity of his subjective development as well as indicating a sense of confidence in his
relationship with English literature, and with the English language. Derrida has made the point, in *Of Spirit*, that the origin of language is responsibility (Derrida, 1989: 132), and
Heaney is discharging his responsibility to a complex sense
of interaction with the English language and culture through
this act of translation and transformation.

His "both/and" philosophy has liberated his sense of self
and he has become able to enter the dialogue between self
and tradition without feeling politically compromised. Instead of seeing *Beowulf* as alien, he can now, at the level of
signifier and signified, posit connections between his own
world and that of the *Beowulf* poet.

As Helen Phillips puts it, the Anglo-Saxon poet's readi-
ness to "contemplate unresolved tensions between the
honour and horror of war and revenge, in his own ancestral
culture", has unmistakable affinities with Heaney's own work
(Phillips, 2001: 265). His *Beowulf* is testimony to that process
of accretion, complexity and above all continuous translation
through which languages, and people, grow and develop. He
is unwilling to see the poem as a historical set-piece; instead
it is translated "as a work of art" which "lives in its own
continuous present, equal to our knowledge of reality in the
present time" (*B*, ix). Even as he takes his sense of Irishness
in an outward-looking direction, so *Beowulf* takes on aspects
of the complex history of Ireland and Britain. It becomes
one of those transformative and complex structures
wherein different strands can co-exist. Hence, he uses the
word "bawn" to refer to Hrothgar's hall, giving the poem a

specifically Irish resonance. In Elizabethan English, this term referred "specifically to the fortified dwellings that the English planters built in Ireland to keep the dispossessed natives at bay". The "entry into a further language" of which he spoke is to be found in the fact that this word ultimately derives from "the Irish *bó-dhún*, a fort for cattle" (*B*, xxx), so the language of the coloniser is implicit in the language of the colonised, an implication that has further consequences for the reading of *Beowulf*. It calls to mind Levinas's statement that "Language is born in responsibility" (Levinas, 1989: 82), implying that the responsibility involved is to the other, to other traditions, other ideas, but most essentially to other people.

Discussing the contemporary value of this poem, Heaney makes this very point. There are resonances between the mindset of the *Beowulf* poet and that of contemporary Northern Ireland. Heaney speaks of:

> the fortuitous correspondence between the in-between condition that the poet occupied in historical time and the in-between condition of our own moment, at the end of the Christian era: what opens up at the end of *Beowulf* is a bewildering vista, a future where all the old securities of the Geat world have been torn away. (Miller, 2000: 43)

He makes the point that while this correspondence is important, what is more important to him — and here we again focus on the importance of the self in the face of social demands and constraints — is the "gravitas of the *Beowulf* poet's mind and the steadiness of his gaze at the bloody realities of face-to-face feuds" (Miller, 2000: 42–3). He goes on to add, significantly, that there is a "rhythm to this discovery of meaning", comparing the connection with *Beowulf* to the earlier connection with the work of Glob, before concluding the point with the following statement: "and then going on to an absorption in it and finally coming through to an act of comprehension, the integration of it into a newer understanding" (Miller, 2000: 43). There are parallels here with the ethical idea of language as a responsibility to the other that we see in the work of Levinas, who posits a mode of critical interpretation which can see art as a "relation with the other" (Levinas, 1989: 143). I would suggest that Heaney's translation of *Beowulf* is an index of such a relation.

As he tells us in "Through-Other Places, Through-Other Times", he first encountered *Beowulf* some forty years earlier as an undergraduate, when it was part of the English canon. He is well aware that his attempts to retell the poem with an Irish inflection can be seen as "exhibiting all the symptoms of the colonial subject". However, Heaney himself was well aware of what a "through-other venture the whole thing would have to be" (*FK*, 381).

Writing about the Anglo-Saxon author Bede, Heaney uses him as a way of expressing his own sense of the value of his translation of Beowulf. Bede tells that scrapings from Irish books, boiled in water, have been known to cure snakebite. Heaney hopes that his translation will function, symbolically, in an analogous manner:

> As an example of a writer calling upon a fiction in order to cope with differences between the two islands linked and separated in various degrees by history and geography, language and culture. As such it prefigures much of the work that would be done by Irish poets in the coming times and much that will continue to be done. (*FK*, 382)

This work will help achieve his sense of a new understanding.

This "newer understanding", achieved through the absorption and transforming of other texts from other cultures, is an analogue of the poetic processes which we have been describing. It involves that sense of openness to out-

ITEMS ON ISSUE
FOR Paul Davis
ON 15/11/11 16:11:45

05/11776709002
Friel Brian
Plays:1 Philadelphia Here I Come!;The Fr
Issued 07/11/11 12:26:53
Renewed
        Count 1 (1 unseen)
Due   12/12/11

DLR20000126628
O'Brien Eugene
Seamus Heaney creating Irelands of the m
Issued 15/11/11 16:11:28
Due   07/12/11

side influences, and an ability to see connections and to create a sufficiently fluid intellectual structure which will allow those connections to be integrated into the self. The use of a "bawn" in *Beowulf* has a further layer of meaning for Heaney, as in his first prose collection, *Preoccupations*, he spoke of the name of his own home in terms which are similar to what we have been discussing.

Writing of "Mossbawn" he explained that:

> Our farm was called Mossbawn. *Moss*, a Scots word probably carried to Ulster by the Planters, and *bawn*, the name the English colonists gave to their fortified farmhouses. Mossbawn, the planter's house on the bog. Yet in spite of this Ordinance Survey spelling, we pronounced it Moss bann, and *Bán* is the Gaelic word for white. So might not the thing mean the white moss, the moss of bog-cotton? In the syllables of my home I see a metaphor of the split culture of Ulster. Mossbawn lies between the villages of Castledawson and Toome. I was symbolically placed between the marks of English influence and the lure of the native experience, between "the demesne" and "the bog". (*P*, 35)

This notion of being "between" both cultures has long been clear in his poetry. In *Preoccupations*, from the very early essays, he looks towards his own writing as a source of healing, a healing which is located in his own individual consciousness. He is well aware that it is through symbol, myth and language that the adversarial positions of nationalism and unionism are perpetuated, so he sets out to seek that "further language", that "newer understanding", which would try to heal that rift, to form some sort of connection between the two experiences:

> I began as a poet when my roots were crossed with my reading. I think of the personal and Irish pieties

> as vowels, and the literary awarenesses nourished on
> English as consonants. My hope is that the poems
> will be vocables adequate to my whole experience.
> (*P*, 37)

As Anne Stevenson has put it, out of the "conscious and
unconscious hemispheres of experience he has constructed
a habitable inner world which we may call understanding"
(Stevenson, 2001: 137). The idea of poems as being fusions
of the contending factors of his experience is important as,
from the outset, Heaney has been creating formal structures
whose function was the integration and dynamic interaction
of contending forces and traditions. In the light of the above
definition, every word he writes is a form of "further language", a way of encouraging the self towards that further
shore in order to make it "allthroughother".

   In another essay in *Preoccupations*, "Feeling into Words",
he speaks about another structure which he hopes to create
in his poetry:

> I mean that I felt it imperative to discover a field of
> force in which, without abandoning fidelity to the
> processes and experience of poetry as I have out-
> lined them, it would be possible to encompass the
> perspectives of a humane reason and at the same
> time to grant the religious intensity of the violence
> its deplorable authenticity and complexity. (*P*, 56–7)

Heaney's field of force, like his notion of the vocable, involves this crossing and interaction of languages and cultures. It sees both language and culture as open to all sorts
of influences. It does not fear change, but rather, leaves open
a landing space for that change to happen. In this respect, it
is similar to Walter Benjamin's and Theodore Adorno's notion of a constellation. This term is best understood in
terms of the homology "ideas are to objects as constella-

tions are to stars" (Benjamin, 1977: 34). The constellation is a model of a fluid structure which allows for the interaction of different elements. It consists of a series of juxtaposed clusters of changing elements that, according to Martin Jay: "resist reduction to a common denominator, essential core, or generative first principle" (Jay, 1984: 15). Such structures, implicit in his poetry through the image clusters we have been tracing, are rendered explicit in his prose, as he constantly returns to such structural tropes to explain his ideas about the relationship between self and other.

His notion of the twin meanings of "Mossbawn" is itself part of a force field where both traditions are, in different ways, at home in the word; just as in *Beowulf*, an essentially Irish word, *bawn*, which has taken on a colonial connotative meaning, is now placed in a new structure wherein it resonates with the Anglo-Saxon context. We have already noted Heaney's comments on "From the Frontier of Writing" where he speaks of the "inquisition and escape and freedom implicit in a certain kind of lyric poem" (Foster, 1989: 132). Rather than being a barrier between cultures, Heaney's placement of the different meanings in his force field means that these differences allow for that process of interrogation and investigation that have been important in his development as a writer.

This preoccupation with structure is further explored in his collection *The Redress of Poetry*, in the final essay entitled "Frontiers of Writing", where he speaks about a structure called the "quincunx", which in many ways solidifies the earlier field of force notion. As we have seen from his poetry, he is acutely conscious of the different strands that are woven together to construct an identity. In a specifically Irish context, he sets out the parameters in a five-point structure which would grant the plurality of what he terms an Irishness that "would not prejudice the rights of others' Britishness" (*RP*, 198). In his quincunx, he traces out a structure with five towers, the central one being "the tower of prior Irelandness, the round tower of insular dwelling" (*RP*, 199). Interestingly, this is the mode of identity which his first four books, *Wintering Out* and *North* specifically, attempted to enunciate. It is a measure of how far Heaney has come, and how those "curt cuts of an edge" have deracinated his thought process, that it is now just one among five points of an interactive constellation of identity in his quincunx.

At the southern point of " a diamond shape" he places Kilcolman castle, Edmund Spenser's tower, "the tower of English conquest and the Anglicization of Ireland, linguistically, culturally, institutionally". In the western side he places Yeats's Ballylee, where the "Norman tower" was a deliberate symbol of his attempt to "restore the spiritual values and magical world-view that Spenser's armies and language had destroyed", though the fact that it is a "Norman" tower further complicates the structural matrix. The fourth tower, on the east, is, of course, Joyce's Martello tower:

> the setting of the opening chapter of *Ulysses* and symbol of Joyce's attempt to "Hellenize the island", his attempt to marginalize the imperium which had marginalized him by replacing the Anglocentric Protestant tradition with a newly forged apparatus of Homeric correspondences, Dantesque scholasticism and a more or less Mediterranean, European, classically endorsed world-view. (*RP*, 199)

The northern tower, Carrickfergus Castle, associated with Louis MacNeice, is where William of Orange once landed in Ireland.

However, the important part of this structure is its many internal dynamics and crossings. In a passage beginning with that now emblematic Heaneyism "so", he makes this point clearly:

> So: we can say that Spenser's tower faces in to the
> round tower of the mythic first Irish place and sees
> popery, barbarism and the Dark Ages; Yeats's tower
> faces it and sees a possible unity of being, an Irish na-
> tion retrieved and enabled by a repossession of its
> Gaelic heritage; Joyce's tower faces it and sees an
> archetypal symbol, the *omphalos*, the navel of a rein-
> vented order, or maybe the ivory tower from which
> the chaste maid of Irish Catholic provincialism must
> be liberated into the secular freedoms of Europe.
> (*RP*, 199–200)

One could amplify this passage by imagining how each of the
other towers would look from any of the perspectives being
outlined, and a diagrammatic representation (alas, beyond
the proficiency of the present author!) would demonstrate a
nexus of intersecting lines. It is in these intersections, I
would argue, that Heaney's quincunx has its meaning — it is
the apotheosis of the earlier notion of a field of force, as
different strands come into contact, and, possibly, to a new
understanding of each other. Clearly, the quincunx as a
whole would signify different notions of identity from each
of the different perspectives. In such a structure, as we see:
"the univocal meaning of each element is continually cor-
rected and altered" (Levinas, 1989: 146), and as such, it is
emblematic of the imperative that we have seen at work in
Heaney's writing. "Irishness", as such, will be defined differently by different groups, and from different perspectives.

In the person of Louis MacNeice, Heaney would seem to
be suggesting an avatar of this form of identity, one with
connections to Spenser, through literature, Yeats through
Connemara, and Joyce through a European idea of myth:

> He can be regarded as an Irish Protestant writer
> with Anglocentric attitudes who managed to be

faithful to his Ulster inheritance, his Irish affections
and his English predilections. (*RP*, 200)

This is a clearly thought-out notion of the complexities of
identity in a literary context, and it is very much in keeping
with what Heaney has seen as the role of the poet. Writing
in the title essay, he describes the expectation of a culture
on its artists at a time of crisis. Taking three examples, an
English poet in the First World War, an Irish poet in the
wake of the 1916 Rising and an American poet during the
Vietnam War, he notes that the cultural expectations on
each would be broadly similar. In the First World War, they
would be to contribute to the war effort by "dehumanizing
the face of the enemy" (*RP*, 2); in 1916, to "revile the tyr-
anny of the executing power"; and in the Vietnam War, to
"wave the flag rhetorically" (*RP*, 3). These are very much the
pressures felt by the early Heaney, and discussed in his poetry. His answer underlines his notion of one of the re-
dresses of poetry, as it can see the German soldier "as a
friend"; the British Government as a body "which might
keep faith" and Vietnam as an "imperial betrayal". To take
any of these perspectives "is to add a complication where
the general desire is for a simplification" (*RP*, 3).

It is this need to go beyond simplification that is so important in Heaney's writing. His thoughts on the value of
poetry can be brought to this conclusion: it has to be "a
working model of inclusive consciousness. It should not simplify" (*RP*, 8). It must be true to the complexities of modern,
or postmodern life, and as such, Heaney's work parallels the
growing complexity of life, political, social, religious and cultural, in contemporary Ireland.

Thus, in his first collection, *Preoccupations*, he spoke of
the influence of Kavanagh, Hopkins and Eliot, as well as providing vivid descriptions of the actuality of the violence in
Northern Ireland. However, in his second collection, *The*

Government of the Tongue, these are gradually enfolded by a more cosmopolitan range of figures: Chekhov, Osip and Nadezhda Mandelstam, Miroslav Holub, Zbiegniew Herbert, figures who in turn inspire a revisitation and revision of the original preoccupations. In the title essay, where he discusses the different meaning of the phrase "government of the tongue", he invokes Osip Mandelstam to criticise "the purveyors of ready-made meaning" (*GT*, 91). Heaney's increasing invocation of Eastern European exemplars has been a fruitful example of his development, as through an examination of the pressure on these writers from political sources, and of their responses to that pressure, a new paradigm came into being.

It is worth keeping in mind that, in *Preoccupations*, his model for poetry was organic: he saw poetry, hardly surprisingly, as a "dig, a dig for finds that end up being plants" (*P*, 41). Through his looking outward towards other writers, this organicist perspective ceases to be the guiding metaphor, and instead takes its place in an evolving aesthetic structure. Now, in "The Government of the Tongue", he probes the ambiguity that is at the very nature of this phrase, and by extension the role of poetry itself. He sees the idea as referring to an aspect of "poetry as its own vindicating force", noting that the "poetic art is credited with an authority of its own" (*GT*, 92). The organic perspective is now subsumed in a more complicated interaction between poetry and reality: "the order of art becomes an achievement intimating a possible order beyond itself, although its relation to that further order remains promissory rather than obligatory" (*GT*, 94). Of course, the phrase "govern your tongue" can also mean a denial of "the tongue's autonomy and permission" (*GT*, 96), in the face of an authoritarian regime which fears "the subversive and necessary function of writing as truth-telling" (*GT*, 97). This more complicated relationship between the aesthetic and politic is part of that process of development that we have been analysing. Its role is not merely to reinforce reality but to be a voice which acts at a tangent (and here, we hear again the voice of the Joycean avatar in "Station Island").

As Heaney puts it later in the book, a poem "floats adjacent to, parallel to, the historical moment" (*GT*, 121). The poet's role is not to use his gift as a slingstone for the desperate or for any other group. Instead it is, in the words of Zbigniew Herbert, concerned with salvaging "out of the catastrophe of history at least two words, without which all poetry is an empty play of meanings and appearances, namely: justice and truth" (*GT*, xviii). For Heaney, that promissory relationship is encapsulated in the injunction to enjoy poetry "as long as you don't use it to escape reality" (*GT*, xix). Highly conscious as he is of the connotative and denotative meanings of language, especially in an ideologically charged arena such as Northern Ireland, he feels that it is only through language that some form of direction, that loophole of which he spoke in the *Beowulf* introduction, can be found towards that "further language" which is his goal.

The example of Eastern European poets was salutary in this process, as their experience makes them "attractive to a reader whose formative experiences have been largely Irish":

> There is an unsettled aspect to the different worlds they inhabit, and one of the challenges they face is to survive amphibiously, in the realm of "the times" and the realm of their moral and artistic self-respect. (*GT*, xx)

Poetry can help this process of amphibious survival, and in his Nobel Prize lecture, *Crediting Poetry*, Heaney makes this very point:

> I credit it ultimately because poetry can make an or-
> der as true to the impact of external reality and as
> sensitive to the inner laws of the poet's being as the
> ripples that rippled in and rippled out across the wa-
> ter in that scullery bucket fifty years ago. An order
> where we can at last grow up to that which we
> stored up as we grew. An order which satisfies all
> that is appetitive in the intelligence and prehensile in
> the affections. I credit poetry, in other words, both
> for being itself and for being a help, for making pos-
> sible a fluid and restorative relationship between the
> mind's centre and its circumference. (*CP*, 11–12)

Here, the focus is completely on the individual complex self,
and on the credit that should be given to poetry for such
development. Significantly, the focus is also on poetry as a
relationship between different areas of that self, symbolised
by the ripples across the water, yet another image of water
as a salvific force in Heaney's writing.

His lecture ends with the assertion of the value of the
aesthetic as a force for moral and ethical good within the
consciousness of the individual:

> The form of the poem, in other words, is crucial to
> poetry's power to do the thing which always is and
> always will be to poetry's credit: the power to per-
> suade that vulnerable part of our consciousness of its
> rightness in spite of the evidence of wrongness all
> around it, the power to remind us that we are hunt-
> ers and gatherers of values, that our very solitudes
> and distresses are creditable, in so far as they, too,
> are an earnest of our veritable human being. (*CP*, 29)

For Heaney, this is the ultimate value of poetry: its ability to
act as a tuning fork for our individual ethics and choices, as
well as being a source of pleasure in itself. For him, it is language working at its most human pitch. It allows for the

mind to imagine a reality that is better. Even in the face of a reality which denies all of these values, and which attempts to simplify issues of value and ethics to authoritarian mantras, poetry will always speak to the inner voice.

The sight of an Irish writer confidently taking his place on the podium at Stockholm, having his poems cited for their lyrical beauty and ethical depth, exemplifies just how much Heaney has developed, and how well he represents the new Ireland of the third millennium. This Ireland, while still conscious of the past, is unwilling to see the narrative of that past as a point of closure. Instead, this past is renegotiated, in a manner outlined in the structure of the quincunx, with other versions of the past. To return to *Beowulf*:

> Putting a bawn into *Beowulf* seems one way for an Irish poet to come to terms with that complex history of conquest and colony, absorption and resistance, integrity and antagonism, a history that has to be clearly acknowledged by all concerned in order to render it ever more "willable forward / again and again and again". (*B*, xxx)

His 2001 collection, *Electric Light*, sustains and further develops this new understanding.

Chapter Six

Electric Light

The Ireland of the twenty-first century is vastly different to the Ireland in which Heaney began to write in the 1960s. We are more open, more multicultural and far more confident in our ability to compete on equal terms with the rest of Europe and the world. Culturally, our writers and artists can justly claim to be at the forefront of the world stage. Poets, novelists, playwrights and filmmakers have achieved great success over the past twenty years, and Irish cultural entertainment has never been more popular, or more central in terms of its importance. No longer relegated to a sub-genre of Anglo-Irish writing, Irish writing has now assumed centre stage. The corollary of this process is that Irish writing, while still occupied with Irish themes, has assumed a more Eurocentric perspective, looking towards European and world literature to provide images, analogues and a broader outlook on those themes.

We have seen how Heaney has gradually included more and more outward references in his work, with his Merriman–Ovid comparison as symbolic of a greater sense of confidence in our own literature as part of a "new commonwealth of art" (*OL*, 9). This confidence allows Irish writing to see itself as being part of "world literature" (*GT*, 31) and, by extension, allows the Irish psyche to forget any postcolonial feelings of inadequacy. It also puts the ongoing Irish–British relationship in its place as part, and only part, of our history, and an even smaller part of our future. It is in the context of such reimagining that we will examine Seamus Heaney's most recent collection, *Electric Light*.

Electric Light has been the subject of a number of reviews since its publication, many of which can be seen to damn the book with faint praise. John Carey, one of Heaney's strongest critical supporters in the past, has made the point that this is Heaney's "most literary collection to date — which may disconcert his admirers". He goes on: "caring about life, especially primitive rural life, rather than literature has always seemed a hallmark of his poetic integrity" (Carey, 2001: 35). Such a reading is quite commonplace among Heaney criticism, and it seems to me that it is stuck in a sort of critical time-warp, as it misses the growing surety of tone, theme and allusive range that is the hallmark of Heaney's later poetry. Such a perspective ignores the fact that Heaney has always been a highly intertextual and allusive poet. Indeed, I would argue that what connects the later books is a thematic and allusive nexus of classical imagery, translations from Irish, Anglo-Saxon and Greek, an increasing focus on the present and future, as opposed to the past, and a concentration on the personal as opposed to the communal — developments encapsulated in the lines: "Me waiting till I was fifty / To credit marvels" (*ST*, 50).

Electric Light is a book which revisits many of Heaney's old topics and themes but in a manner which complicates and deepens the psychic material and which considerably enhances the Heaney canon. Given the early use of place-names in his poetry, and given the specific use of "Toome" in *Wintering Out*, the opening poem, "At Toombridge" is almost a *recherche du temps perdu*, as he revisits the earlier poem where the sound of the word conjured up images of the Irish past — "loam, flints, musket-balls" — and saw him imaginatively immersed in "bogwater and tributaries, / and elvers tail my hair" (*WO*, 26). In the new poem, the river is seen as the "continuous / Present" while the past is no longer mythological but quantifiable. He refers to where "the checkpoint used to be" and to the "rebel boy" who was hanged in 1798, but goes on to stress the new importance of "negative ions in the open air" which are "poetry to me". This is an important point, as it is the negative and the present that will be the inspiration of this book, as opposed to the "slime and silver of the fattened eel" which were inspirations "before" (*EL*, 3). He is taking his inheritance and making it "willable forward".

This concentration on the present and the future, at the expense of the past, extrapolates from a thematic movement in the later books, as he focuses on the "music of what might happen". It becomes a recurrent *topos* throughout the book, as he speaks about the "everything flows and steady go of the world" (*EL*, 4), or the "erotics of the future" (*EL*, 5) or "a span of pure attention" (*EL*, 54). The book embraces the ordinary, endowing it with a significance of memory and hindsight. Thus, he can speak of the courting days of himself and his wife Marie, in a poem entitled "Red, White and Blue", a title which immediately raises expectations of a political subtext, suggesting the colours of the British Union Jack or the Stars and Stripes. Instead, he eschews the political in favour of the personal, referring to the colours of different clothes worn by his wife, Marie, at different stages of their life together: a "much-snapped scarlet coat" (*EL*, 28); a "cut-off top" in the labour ward, of "White calico" (*EL*, 29) and a "blue denim skirt / And denim jacket" (*EL*, 30). This favouring of the personal over the political is another sign of his progression, as it is his personal and familial past which is now important, as opposed to the old flags and banners. The touch here is just right, remembering someone's description

of her walk — "She's like a wee pony" — and of his own
irritated reaction to such a description:

> I love the go and gladsomeness in her,
> Something unbroken, her gift for pure dismay
> At shits like you. (*EL*, 28)

The second section is a birth poem, recalling the less successful "Act of Union" in *North*. Heaney, in common with
other fathers of his time, was not present at the birth of his
child. The location of the hospital next to a swimming pool
is caught by the phrase "banshee acoustic" (*EL*, 28), while
the extended metaphor of the speaker as a knight-errant
reaches a bathetic climax as he pictures "the Knight of the
White Feather turning tail" from the labour ward (*EL*, 29).
The unsentimental and wryly mocking note of this conveys a
sense of ease as he recalls all aspects of his past life, without
the need to over-dramatise or sentimentalise the birth of his
child. The final section recalls a young Heaney and Marie,
hitchhiking in the Republic of Ireland, meeting a "*veh*" British
couple who were admiring the "gate-lodge and the avenue /
At Castlebellingham". This memory stirs a further memory
of Marie in "a Fair Isle tank-top and blue denim skirt", calling
her a "Botticelli dressed down for the sixties" (*EL*, 30).

   This image, a syncretism of Irish and classical, is a synecdoche of the main thrust of this book, and I would suggest,
of his *oeuvre* as a whole — the fusion and interaction of Irish
and European culture. Oddly enough, this European dimension, flagged by an unusually large amount of literary and linguistic allusion, brings Heaney full circle in terms of his own
poetic development. In an essay entitled "Learning from
Eliot", delivered as the *Cheltenham Lecture* in October 1988,
Heaney spoke of his early experiences of the work of Eliot.
He saw the *Collected Poems* as the "first 'grown up' books"
he owned (*LE*, 17), but rather than being an inspiration, the
book represented Heaney's sense of "distance" from the

mystery of literature (*LE*, 18). The early Heaney was stylisti-
cally and culturally far removed from Eliot, and yet in *Electric
Light*, the polyglot allusiveness of *The Waste Land* hovers
over Heaney's writing. Indeed, there is a sly homage to *The
Waste Land* in "Vitruviana", where, Eliot's lines from "The
Fire Sermon" —

> On Margate Sands
> I can connect
> Nothing with nothing. (Eliot, 1963: 74)

— find an allusive analogue in Heaney's:

> On Sandymount strand I can connect
> Some bits and pieces. (*EL*, 53)

The title of this poem is similarly allusive, referring to the
style of Vitruvius, a Roman architect and writer of the first
century BC, whose book *De Architectura* was later influential
in the development of Renaissance architecture. It is this
process of influence and mutual transformation that is at the
core of the book. He has taken even more from the literature of the European past, and by inserting it in his own
work, has transformed aspects of his own work, through
this further language.

Indeed, one could go so far as to say that it is this construction of a series of intercultural and interlinguistic connections that is the underlying imperative of this book. It is
worth examining the number of foreign words, phrases, literary allusions and generally cosmopolitan references that
are to be found studded throughout the poems. A casual
glance reveals references to Asclepius (*EL*, 7); Epidaurus (*EL*,
8); Hygeia (*EL*, 9); Virgil (*EL*, 11); Grendel (*EL*, 18); El Greco
(*EL*, 22); Lycidas, Moeris (*EL*, 31) as well as a pantheon of
modern English, American and European writers — Friel,
Dante, Auden, Wilfred Owen, Ted Hughes, Czeslaw Miłosz,
Joseph Brodsky, Zbigniew Herbert, George MacKay Brown

. . . the list goes on. Linguistically, we see snatches of Latin (*poeta doctus* (*EL*, 7); *miraculum* (*EL*, 8); *carmen, ordo, nascitur, saeculum, gens* (*EL*, 11); *Pacatum orbem* (*EL*, 12); *rigor vitae* (*EL*, 14); *in medias res* (*EL*, 24)); Macedonian (*Nema problema* (*EL*, 19)); German (*ja* (*EL*, 23)); French (*de haut en bas* (*EL*, 23)); Italian (*Godi, fanciullo mio; stato soave* (*EL*, 26)); and Irish (*cailleach*; *Slieve na mBard, Knock Filiocht, Ben Duan* (*EL*, 43)). It is as if the gradual allusiveness that we have traced through his other books has suddenly burst forth in all its glory. To borrow from the metaphor of the book's title, it is as if a switch had been turned on by a *poeta doctus*.

In addition to this cosmopolitan range of literary and linguistic allusion, there is also a strain of reference to other languages and literatures running through the titles of the poems, as a glance at the Contents will reveal: "Montana" (*EL*, 13), "The Little Canticles of Asturias" (*EL*, 24), "Virgil: Eclogue IX" (*EL*, 31), "Sonnets from Hellas" (*EL*, 38), "Vitruviana" (*EL*, 53), "Arion" (*EL*, 72). There is also a series of elegies for writers from different traditions: "On His Work in the English Tongue" (Ted Hughes) (*EL*, 61); "Audenesque" (Joseph Brodsky) (*EL*, 64); "To the Shade of Zbigniew Herbert" (*EL*, 67); "Would They Had Stay'd" (a series of British poets) (*EL*, 68); "Late in the Day" (David Thomson) (*EL*, 70). These are intermingled with elegies for friends who have died: Rory Kavanagh (*EL*, 75) and Mary Ó Muirithe (*EL*, 77).

However, in keeping with the structural matrix which we have been tracing, intersecting with this cosmopolitan range of names and places, there are a number of local names and places which take their place in this constellation: Toombridge, the Bann, Lough Neagh, Butler's Bridge, St Columb's College, Ballynahinch Lake, Dr Kerlin, John Dologhan, Bob Cushley, Ned Kane, Owen Kelly, Gerry O'Neill, as well as those remembered in elegies. What the book achieves is the placement of these different cultures in the same structure, so that each can maintain its integrity while, in the manner of the quincunx, also create the conditions for change. This is clear from much of "The Real Names", but specifically in the lines:

> "Frankie McMahon, you're Bassanio.
> Irwin, Launcelot Gobbo. Bredin, Portia."
> That was the cast, or some of it. (*EL*, 48)

Here, we see the transformation wrought by the literary as imagination allows for such changes: "The smell of the new book. The peep ahead / At words not quite beyond you" (*EL*, 46). In this poem, Heaney charts the power of the literary to change perspective, both in terms of fusing the foreign with the native and in terms of viewing the ordinary in a new light, as when he is "on top of the byre" he sees things in a "headier light that much nearer heaven" (*EL*, 47).

In fact, this is the most overtly "poetic" of all Heaney's books, as the craft of poetry, and the practitioners of that craft, are very much to the fore. The note of guilt or questioning that has so often marked his discussions of the poet and poetry is mitigated here by a sense of confidence in the importance of the craft. Thus, when in the persona of an Anglo-Saxon poet being taken to task because his "first and last" lines of a poem were "Neither here nor there", the reply is the wry: "Since when . . . Are the first line and last line of any poem / Where the poem begins and ends?" (*EL*, 57). In his elegy for Ted Hughes, "On His Work in the English Tongue", he begins with the declarative:

> Post-this, post-that, post-the-other, yet in the end
> Not past a thing. Not understanding or telling
> Or forgiveness. (*EL*, 61)

Having rehearsed an episode from *Beowulf*, he concludes with Miłosz's definition of poetry as a "dividend from ourselves", which he amplifies as "a tribute paid / By what we have been true to. A thing allowed" (*EL*, 63). The theme of

the Hrethel saga, which appears in *Beowulf*, is "passive suffering", as his younger son accidentally kills his elder son, and
under the law, Hrethel must seek redress for the death, and
watch "his son's body / Swing on the gallows" (*EL*, 62). The
value of poetry, he seems to say, is that it can trace the human dilemmas across the centuries, and perhaps, allow us to
learn from these experiences, or to sympathise with another's sorrow. It is the place, or space, where the "scru-
ples" of the soul can be aired.

His elegy for Joseph Brodsky is completely different in
form and tone, with the regularly constructed quatrains,
each composed of two rhyming couplets, beating out the
metre of the poem. He is writing in the mode of Brodsky,
after Yeats, in a poem entitled "Audenesque":

> Its measured ways I tread again
> Quatrain by constrained quatrain,
> Meting grief and reason out. (*EL*, 64)

His brief elegy for Zbigniew Herbert, one whom "Apollo
favoured", ends on the affirmative line: "You learnt the lyre
from him and kept it tuned" (*EL*, 67), an epitaph worthy of a
writer.

Perhaps the most cosmopolitan poem in the book is the
interestingly titled "Known World", where the opening
quote is in Macedonian, "*Nema problema*" (*EL*, 19), as
Heaney tells of a time, in 1978, when "we hardly ever so-
bered up at the Struga / Poetry festival" (*EL*, 19). The value
of this festival was that Heaney was among fellow poets, at a
time when he was still teaching at Carysfort College. In
other words, he was a part-time poet, who now had a
chance to celebrate the poet's craft: "In Belgrade I had found
my west-in-east", another example of a structure which allows him to make connections between Macedonia of the
1970s and his own childhood Ireland. In ways so familiar, this
experience allowed him to feel that he had "left the known

world" (*EL*, 20), and yet "in that Macedonian poem . . . there
is the flypaper from fifty years ago in the farmhouse in
Mossbawn" (Miller, 2000: 29), symbolic of a different
"known world" of his youth. He felt, in that place, a familiar
"old sense of a tragedy" taking place at the edge of "the
usual", a sensation which remained with him throughout the
visit (*EL*, 21).

He talks of "Hygo Simberg's allegory of Finland", of a
wounded angel "being carried" by "manchild number one"
and "manchild number two", before making a connection
with "another angel, fit as ever, / past each house with a
doorstep daubed 'Serb House'" (*EL*, 21). This sense of sectarian killing has obvious connections with his Northern Irish
experience, while the celebration of poetry with drink indicates the other aspect of the visit. Heaney tells that he felt a
kinship with the people and the "religious subculture that
was still there in the country" (Miller, 2000: 28) as they
celebrated "Greek Orthodox / Madonna's Day": "I had been
there, I knew this, but was still / Haunted by it as by an un-
read dream" (*EL*, 22). Yet he is also at home in the plane
"courtesy of Lufthansa" (*EL*, 22):

> And took it as my due when wine was poured
> By a slight *de haut en bas* of my headphoned head.
> *Nema problema. Ja.* All systems go. (*EL*, 23)

The poem strives to enact that field of force of his developing self, at once at home with a rural pilgrimage, and also
having grown accustomed to frequent air travel: "You want
to be able to include your experience at the circumference
and to find your bearings between the circumference and
the first centre" (Miller, 2000: 29). This poem, like the book,
achieves precisely that. The different experience, different
perspectives, different connections and different languages
signify the openness of the process that allows us to know
different, complementary, worlds.

Perhaps the key thematic element of this book is the fusion of this cosmopolitan and polyglossic range of reference and allusion with the remembered experience of a poet from his own personal past into a structure that is adequate to contemporary Ireland. Thus, in "Out of the Bag", the family doctor who delivered all of the Heaney children, Dr Kerlin, is described in terms of how he appeared to the young Heaney. Given the traditional Irish reticence about matters sexual and gynaecological, the fiction was maintained that "All of us came in Doctor Kerlin's bag", and the accurate adjectival description of the doctor's ministering has all the hallmarks of Heaney's earlier style. However, in describing the doctor's eyes, Heaney uses the slightly unusual adjective "hyperborean", and this word is the hinge, or in Derridean terms, *brisure*, upon which that fusion of Ireland and Classical Europe is achieved. The term refers to a member of a race of people who, in Greek mythology, lived in a land of sunshine and plenty beyond the north wind, worshipping Apollo, and this connection is furthered in the second section where poetry and medicine are also connected through the image of "sanctuaries of Aesclepius" functioning as "the equivalent of hospitals" in ancient Greece, or as "shrines like Lourdes" (*EL*, 7).

This cure by poetry "that cannot be coerced" was reinforced at Epidaurus where Heaney realised that:

> the whole place was a sanatorium
> With theatre and gymnasium and baths,
>
> A site of incubation, where "incubation"
> Was technical and ritual, meaning sleep
> When epiphany occurred and you met the god. (*EL*, 8)

It is such epiphanies that allow the oneiric connection in this poem between Doctor Kerlin, Asclepius and Hygeia, his daughter; between Bellaghy, Epidaurus and Lourdes; between medicine, sleep and poetry; between dream and reality: "The room I came from and the rest of us all came from / Stays pure reality where I stand alone" (*EL*, 9). All are aspects of his field of force, his constellation, and all are granted their place and their transformative potential.

Such epiphany can also be found in his version of Virgil's Eclogue, entitled "Bann Valley *Eclogue*" (one of three such eclogues in the book). Interestingly, the term derives from the Greek "*eklegein*" meaning "to select", and as I have intimated, such a process of selection and combination is at the core of the aesthetic imperative of his work as a whole. All three are dialogue poems where self and other enter an intersubjective discussion which is, in Bakhtinian terms, heteroglossic in that different voices and different languages are allowed to confront each other and achieve some kind of dynamic interaction, or dialogisation (Bakhtin, 1981: 263). It is another birth poem in a book which seems very conscious of the preciousness of birth, both physical and metaphorical. In a poem that has echoes of Yeats's "A Prayer for My Daughter", Heaney hopes to "sing / Better times for her and her generation" (*EL*, 11). It is as if his "cure by poetry" is being slightly coerced in the presence of Virgil. In this colloquy, the voice of Virgil, a *spectator ab extra* on the Northern Irish political situation, posits the cure of poetry, as "whatever stains you, you rubbed it into yourselves / Earth mark, birth mark". Here, he might be back in the territory of *Wintering Out* and *North*, where he spoke, in part, as the voice of his tribe, the *vox loci*. But now, the voice of Virgil suggests a connection between the individual birth and the future:

> But when the waters break
> Bann's stream will overflow, the old markings
> Will avail no more to keep east bank from west.
> The valley will be washed like the new baby. (*EL*, 11)

It is an optimistic forecast, one reined in by the voice of the poet, who warns: "your words are too much nearly" (*EL*, 12). Keeping in mind the meaning of "eclogue", art can choose to look forward or backward, and here the movement is definitely towards an "erotics of the future" as Virgil wishes that the child will "never hear close gunfire or explosion" (*EL*, 12).

These dialogue poems are an important part of his attempt to create that field of force wherein all aspects of identity could have their place and interact. The form recalls Virgil, a presence in one of the poems, and the later Yeats, who also makes effective use of the poetic colloquy to broaden his own range of emotions and voices. The fusion of the classical and the local, both in the title and in the delineation of Virgil as a "hedge-schoolmaster" (*EL*, 11), and in terms of "Glanmore Eclogue", where the poet and his interlocutor discuss "Land commissions making tenants owners" (*EL*, 35), and "peace being talked about" (*EL*, 36), exemplifies what Bakhtin terms *heteroglossia*, the multiplicity of voices that form the modern nation.

His desire to locate himself, and by extension, notions of Irishness, within a broader, outward-looking frame of reference achieves its *telos* in this book. After the first four books, he made the comment that he was now looking for a door into the light, and here, the light is electric. It symbolises the technological advances made in Ireland, advances which he parallels with a growing sense of ease in terms of our sense of being European. *Electric Light* enunciates an intersection of Irish and European cultures, and explores the interstices of the effects of this cross-cultural pollination.

We conclude with the title poem, as for Heaney titles are usually over-determined with respect to their significance within the book. Electric light was brought to Ireland through the Ardnacrusha Power Station, built just after the Irish Civil War, in collaboration with the German engineering firm Siemens. The radical change that this brought to both urban and (especially) rural Ireland was transformative, though such hindsight does not allow for the very real fear that change can bring with it. The fear of change is caught in his fear of the woman and her "voice that at its loudest did nothing else / But whisper" (*EL*, 80). It is the adult Heaney who can retrospectively see the old woman's house as "a littered Cumae" and speak of her "sibylline English", which is the current that leads him on to a journey, physically, through Belfast Lough to England, and specifically Southwark, a place which, though strange, is seen as familiar in the metaphor "Moyola breath by Thames's 'straunge stronde'" (*EL*, 81). Electric light allows us to see in the dark, to see where we could not see before, to see things anew. *Electric Light* symbolises such a new perspective, as personal, cultural and political events are seen through the alembic of other cultures, literatures and languages in such a way as to see them anew. Home will never be the same again:

> A turn of their wireless knob and light came on
> In the dial. They let me and they watched me
> As I roamed at will the stations of the world. (*EL*, 81)

Ironically, the actual image from "Electric Light" that is most significant here is that of the radio dial, which allows Heaney to experience the different languages and cultures of the world through the radio "stations of the world", a process about which he has spoken so eloquently in his Nobel Prize lecture *Crediting Poetry*, and a process which, I would argue, is developed more fully in this book:

> Now that the other children were older and there was so much going on in the kitchen, I had to get close to the actual radio set in order to concentrate my hearing, and in that intent proximity to the dial I grew familiar with the names of foreign stations, with

Leipzig and Oslo and Stuttgart and Warsaw and, of course, with Stockholm. I also got used to hearing short bursts of foreign languages as the dial hand swept round from BBC to Radio Éireann, from the intonations of London to those of Dublin, and even though I did not understand what was being said in those first encounters with the gutturals and sibilants of European speech, I had already begun a journey into the wideness of the world. This in turn became a journey into the wideness of language, a journey where each point of arrival — whether in one's poetry or one's life — turned out to be a stepping stone rather than a destination, and it is that journey which has brought me now to this honoured spot. And yet the platform here feels more like a space station than a stepping stone, so that is why, for once in my life, I am permitting myself the luxury of walking on air. (*CP*, 10–11)

What is at work here is a parallel process to the development of a new sense of Irishness, an Irishness that is centrifugal as opposed to centripetal in orientation. Here we see an embracing of European and world culture, an unselfconscious placement of Irish experience in the context of such a culture, and a willingness to posit connections between the two. Through electricity, the light of different cultures and languages, the "stations of the world", came into the home and mind of Seamus Heaney, and this is celebrated in the cosmopolitan, sophisticated and nuanced sense of Irishness, as well as in the complexity of identity that is enunciated throughout his writing. The work of Heaney and other Irish poets keeps issues concerning identity, belonging and treatment of other traditions in circulation "at a level of cultural authority, sophistication and subtlety which acts as challenge and affront to the expediency and opportunism of

British and, to a large extent, Irish political consensus" (Corcoran, 1999: 136).

This is very much what we have been tracing in all of Heaney's work. In terms of his achievement, it is probably best summed up by his imagery of translation, of crossing, of the field of force, of space, as he attempts to redefine Irishness in terms of looking outside itself. In an interview, Richard Kearney posed the question as to what it was about the "Mediterranean, southern European experience", especially the "visions and idioms of Homer and Virgil and Dante" that most fascinated Heaney, and his answer describes the very process which we have been examining in terms of the location of Ireland as symbolically a part of Europe:

> I think it's a steadiness and a durability, a sense, for example, that in the word Orpheus, in the word muse, in the word drama, in the word mystery, or whatever, in the etymologies and associations, there is what Louis MacNeice calls a mystical sense of value . . . And I do believe that in the English language, in the French language, in the Italian language, in the Greek language, and I'm sure in many other languages, these deposits do promote a quickening, a challenge. I'm not going to say a transcendent Europe of value, but the possibility of a hopeful, other, renewable, non-utilitarian, joyful spirit of being. Those promises, hopes and invitations reside in that Graeco-Roman-Judaic heritage, I think. (Kearney, 1995: 104)

His teasing out of the requirement that he should speak for his own nationalist community in Northern Ireland — which has developed from a sense of empathy with that tribe ("how we slaughter / for the common good" (*N*, 45)); to a sense of guilt at not being more committed ("Forgive / My timid circumspect involvement" (*FW*, 80)); to a final sense of the value of the individual over the community ("If I do write something / Whatever it is, I'll be writing for myself" (*SL*, 25)) — is of seminal importance to this process.

That sense of self is now conceived as a constellation wherein different experiences between the circumference and the centre can be accommodated. We can do no better than conclude with two of Heaney's own comments on the nature and value of poetry as he understands it, comments that underwrite the perspective which we have been tracing through his work. The first describes what he has learned from T.S. Eliot, comments which have a direct bearing on the themes discussed in this book:

> Perhaps the final thing to be learned is this: in the realm of poetry, as in the realm of consciousness, there is no end to the possible learnings that can take place. Nothing is final, the most gratifying discovery is fleeting, the path of positive achievement leads to the *via negativa*. (*LE*, 30)

The second concludes his essay "The Government of the Tongue":

> Poetry is more a threshold than a path, one constantly approached and constantly departed from, at which reader and writer undergo in their different ways the experience of being summoned and released. (*GT*, 108)

This definition of poetry in terms of a dialectical structure which is constant is very much how Heaney has created his Irelands of the mind.

Select Bibliography

Bibliographical Books and Articles

Brandes, Rand (1994), "Secondary Sources: A Gloss on the Critical Reception of Seamus Heaney, 1965–1993", *Colby Quarterly*, Volume 30, Number 1, pp. 63–77.

Durkan, Michael J and Rand Brandes (1996), *Seamus Heaney: A Reference Guide*, New York: G.K. Hall and Co.

Durkan, Michael J. (1986), "Seamus Heaney: A Checklist for a Bibliography", *Irish University Review*, Vol. 16, No. 1, Spring, pp. 48–76.

Miller, Karl (2000), "Bibliography" in *Seamus Heaney in Conversation with Karl Miller*, London: Between the Lines, pp. 61–101.

Pearson, Henry (1982), "Seamus Heaney: A Bibliographical Checkist", *American Book Collector*, Volume 3, Number 2, March–April, pp. 31–42.

Books and Pamphlets by Seamus Heaney

Heaney, Seamus (1966), *Death of a Naturalist*, London: Faber.

Heaney, Seamus (1969), *Door into the Dark*, London: Faber.

Heaney, Seamus (1972), *Wintering Out*, London: Faber.

Heaney, Seamus (1975), *North*, London: Faber.

Heaney, Seamus (1979), *Field Work*, London: Faber.

186 *Seamus Heaney*

Heaney, Seamus (1980), *Selected Poems 1965–1975*, London: Faber.

Heaney, Seamus (1980), *Preoccupations: Selected Prose 1968–1978*, London: Faber.

Heaney, Seamus (1982), *Verses for a Fordham Commencement*, New York: Fordham University.

Heaney, Seamus (1983), *An Open Letter*, Derry: Field Day.

Heaney, Seamus (1983), *Among Schoolchildren*, Belfast: Queen's University.

Heaney, Seamus (1983), *Sweeney Astray*, Derry: Field Day.

Heaney, Seamus (1984), *Station Island*, London: Faber.

Heaney, Seamus (1985), *Place and Displacement*, Grasmere: Trustees of Dove Cottage.

Heaney, Seamus (1985), "Envies and Identifications: Dante and the Modern Poet", *Irish University Review*, 15 (Spring), pp. 5–19.

Heaney, Seamus (1987), *The Haw Lantern*, London: Faber.

Heaney, Seamus (1988), *The Government of the Tongue: The 1986 T.S. Eliot Memorial Lectures and Other Critical Writings*, London: Faber.

Heaney, Seamus (1989), "Learning from Eliot", in *Agenda: Seamus Heaney Fiftieth Birthday Issue*, pp. 17–31.

Heaney, Seamus (1989), *The Place of Writing*, Atlanta: Scholars Press.

Heaney, Seamus (1989), "Earning a Rhyme", *Poetry Ireland Review*, Ed. John Ennis, No. 25, Spring, pp. 96–100.

Heaney, Seamus (1990), *New Selected Poems 1968–1987*, London: Faber.

Heaney, Seamus (1990), *The Cure at Troy*, London: Faber.

Heaney, Seamus (1991), *Seeing Things*, London: Faber.

Heaney, Seamus (1995), *The Redress of Poetry: Oxford Lectures*, London: Faber.

Heaney, Seamus (1995), *Crediting Poetry*, Oldcastle, County Meath, Ireland: Gallery Press.

Heaney, Seamus (1995), *Laments*, translated by Seamus Heaney and Stanislaw Barańczak, London: Faber.

Heaney, Seamus (1996), *The Spirit Level*, London: Faber.

Heaney, Seamus (1996), "The Frontier of Writing", in Jacqueline Genet and Wynne Hellegouarc'h (eds.), *Irish Writers and their Creative Process*, London: Colin Smythe, pp. 3–16.

Heaney, Seamus (1999), *Beowulf*, London: Faber.

Heaney, Seamus (1999), "Translating Beowulf", *Times Literary Supplement*, 12 November, pp. 14–15.

Heaney, Seamus (2000), *The Midnight Verdict*, Oldcastle, County Meath, Ireland: Gallery Press.

Heaney, Seamus (2001), *Electric Light*, London: Faber.

Heaney, Seamus (2005), *The Door Stands Open: Czesław Miłosz 1911–2004*, Dublin: Irish Writers' Centre.

Heaney, Seamus (2005), "Thebes Via Toomebridge: Retitling *Antigone*", *The Irish Book Review*, Vol. 1, No. 1 (Spring), pp. 12–14.

Interviews with Seamus Heaney

Broadbridge, Edward (1977), Radio Interview with Seamus Heaney, published in *Seamus Heaney Skoleradioen*, Copenhagen: Danmarks Radio, pp. 5–16.

Deane, Seamus (1977), "Unhappy and at home: interview with Seamus Heaney", *The Crane Bag Book of Irish Studies*, Dublin: Blackwater Press (1982), pp. 66–72.

Deane, Seamus (1979), "Talk with Seamus Heaney", *New York Times Book Review*, LXXXIV, 48 (December 2), pp. 79–101.

Donnelly, Brian (1977), Interview with Seamus Heaney, *Seamus Heaney Skoleradioen* Broadbridge, Edward (ed.), (1977), Copenhagen: Danmarks Radio, pp. 59–61.

Farndale, Nigel (2001), "The poet, his father, the Provos and the glittering prizes", *Irish Independent* (April 21), pp. 8–10.

Haffenden, John (1981), "Meeting Seamus Heaney: An Interview", *Viewpoints: Poets in Conversation*, London: Faber, pp. 57–75.

Kearney, Richard (1995), "Seamus Heaney — Between North and South: poetic detours", *States of Mind: Dialogues with contemporary thinkers on the European mind*, Manchester: Manchester University Press, pp. 101–108.

Kinahan, Frank (1982), "Artists on Art: An Interview with Seamus Heaney", *Critical Inquiry*, VIII, 3, pp. 405–414.

Miller, Karl (2000), *Seamus Heaney in Conversation with Karl Miller*, London: Between the Lines.

Murphy, Mike (2000b), *Reading the Future: Irish Writers in Conversation with Mike Murphy*, Dublin: Lilliput Press, pp. 81–98.

Mooney, Bel (1988), Interview with Seamus Heaney, *Turning Points*, British Broadcasting Corporation.

Randall, James (1979), "An Interview with Seamus Heaney", *Ploughshares*, Vol. 5, No. 3, pp. 7–22.

Walsh, Caroline (1975), "Saturday Interview: Caroline Walsh talks to Seamus Heaney", *Irish Times*, 6 December, p. 5.

White, Barry (1989), "Interview with Seamus Heaney", *Belfast Telegraph*, 29 June, p. 9.

Books on the Writing of Seamus Heaney

Allen, Michael (ed.) (1997), *Seamus Heaney*, New Casebook Series, London: Macmillan.

Andrews, Elmer (1988), *The Poetry of Seamus Heaney: All the Realms of Whisper*, London: Macmillan.

Andrews, Elmer (ed.) (1998), *The Poetry of Seamus Heaney*, Icon Critical Guides Series, Cambridge: Icon Books.

Annwn, David (1984), *Inhabited Voices: Myth and History in the Poetry of Geoffrey Hill, Seamus Heaney and George Mackay Brown*, Somerset: Bran's Head Books.

Bloom, Harold (ed.), (1986), *Seamus Heaney*, Modern Critical Views Series, New Haven: Chelsea House Publishers.

Brandes, Rand and Michael J. Durkan (1994), *Seamus Heaney: A Reference Guide*, New York: G.K. Hall.

Broadbridge, Edward (ed.) (1977), *Seamus Heaney: Skoleradioen*, Copenhagen: Danmarks Radio.

Burris, Sidney (1990), *The Poetry of Resistance: Seamus Heaney and the Pastoral Tradition*, Athens: Ohio University Press.

Buttel, Robert (1975), *Seamus Heaney*, Lewisburg: Bucknell University Press.

Byron, Catherine (1992), *Out of Step: Pursuing Seamus Heaney to Purgatory*, Bristol: Loxwood Stoneleigh.

Cookson, William and Dale, Peter (eds.) (1989), *Agenda: Seamus Heaney Fiftieth Birthday Issue*, Vol. 27, No. 1, London: Agenda and Editions Charitable Trust.

Corcoran, Neil (1998), *Seamus Heaney*, London: Faber (First published in 1986).

Corcoran, Neil (1999), *Poets of Modern Ireland: Text, Context, Intertext*, Cardiff: University of Wales Press.

Corcoran, Neil (ed.) (2000), *The Chosen Ground: Essays on the Contemporary Poetry of Northern Ireland*, Bridgend, Mid Glamorgan: Poetry Wales Press.

Curtis, Tony (ed.) (2001), *The Art of Seamus Heaney*, Dublin: Wolfhound Press (Fourth revised edition; Originally published by Poetry Wales Press, 1982).

Fennell, Desmond (1991), *Whatever You Say, Say Nothing*, Dublin: ELO Publications.

Foster, T.C. (1989), *Seamus Heaney*, Dublin: O'Brien Press.

Garratt, Robert F. (ed.), (1995), *Critical Essays on Seamus Heaney*, London: Prentice Hall.

Hart, Henry (1992), *Seamus Heaney: Poet of Contrary Progressions*, New York: Syracuse University Press.

Haviaras, Stratis (ed.) (1996), *Seamus Heaney: A Celebration*, A Harvard Review Monograph, Cambridge, MA: The President and Fellows of Harvard College.

Lloyd, David (1993), "'Pap for the Dispossessed': Seamus Heaney and the Poetics of Identity" in *Anomalous States: Irish Writing and the Postcolonial Moment*, Dublin: Lilliput, pp. 13–40.

Maguire, Aisling (1986), *Seamus Heaney: York Notes on Selected Poems*, Essex: Longman.

Malloy, Catharine and Carey, Phyllis (1996), *Seamus Heaney: The Shaping Spirit*, Newark: University of Delaware Press.

Mathews, Steven (1997), *Irish Poetry: Politics, History, Negotiation: The Evolving Debate 1969 to the Present*, London: Macmillan.

McDonald, Peter (1997), *Mistaken Identities: Poetry and Northern Ireland*, Oxford: Clarendon Press.

McGuinn, Nicholas (1986), *Seamus Heaney: A Student's Guide to the Selected Poems 1965–1975*, Leeds: Arnold Wheaton.

McGuckian, Medhb (1999), *Horsepower Pass By! A Study of the Car in the Poetry of Seamus Heaney*, Coleraine: Cranagh Press.

Morrison, Blake (1982), *Seamus Heaney*, London: Methuen.

Molino, Michael (1994), *Questioning Tradition, Language and Myth: The Poetry of Seamus Heaney*, Washington DC: Catholic University Press.

Murphy, Andrew (2000a), *Seamus Heaney*, Writers and Their Work Series, Plymouth: Northcote House in association with the British Council (First published in 1996).

O'Donoghue, Bernard (1994), *Seamus Heaney and the Language of Poetry*, Hemel Hempstead: Harvester Wheatsheaf.

Oeser, Hans-Christian (ed.) (1994), *Transverse II: Seamus Heaney in Translation*, Irish Translators' Association, pp. 83–96.

Parker, Michael (1993), *Seamus Heaney: The Making of a Poet*, Dublin: Gill and Macmillan.

Ramazani, Jahan (1994), *Poetry of Mourning: The Modern Elegy from Hardy to Heaney*, Chicago: University of Chicago Press.

Tamplin, Ronald (1989), *Seamus Heaney*, Milton Keynes: Open University Press.

Tobin, Daniel (1998), *Passage to the Center: Imagination and the Sacred in the Poetry of Seamus Heaney*, Lexington: University Press of Kentucky.

Vendler, Helen (1995), *The Breaking of Style: Hopkins, Heaney, Graham*, Cambridge, MA: Harvard University Press.

Vendler, Helen (1998), *Seamus Heaney*, London: Harper Collins.

Wade, Stephen (1993), *More on the Word-Hoard: The Work of Seamus Heaney*, Nottingham: Pauper's Press.

Warren, Rosanna (ed.), *The Art of Translation: Voices from the Field*, Boston: Northeastern University Press: 13–20.

Wilson Foster, John (1995), *The Achievement of Seamus Heaney*, Dublin: Lilliput Press.

Articles & Essays on Heaney's Work in Books & Journals

Allen, Michael (1988), "'Holding Course': *The Haw Lantern* and its Place in Heaney's Development", *The Irish Review*, 3, pp. 108–118 (Reprinted in Andrews (ed.) (1992), *Seamus Heaney: A Collection of Critical Essays*, London: Macmillan, pp. 193–207).

Bailey, Anthony (1980), *Acts of Union: Reports from Ireland*, London: Faber, pp. 123–138.

Brown, Terence (1992), "The Witnessing Eye and the Speaking Tongue", in Elmer Andrews (ed.) (1992), *Seamus Heaney: A Collection of Critical Essays*, London: Macmillan, pp. 182–192.

Carey, John (2001), "Going Back to his Roots", Review of *Electric Light*, *The Sunday Times*, Culture supplement, pp. 35–36.

Carson, Ciarán (1975), "Escaped from the Massacre?", *The Honest Ulsterman*, 50 (Winter), pp. 183–186.

Carson, Ciarán (2001), "*Sweeney Astray*: Escaping from Limbo", in Tony Curtis, *The Art of Seamus Heaney* (see separate entry), pp. 139–148.

Coughlin, Patricia (1997), "'Bog Queens': The Representation of Women in the Poetry of John Montague and Seamus Heaney", in Michael Allen (ed.), *Seamus Heaney: New Casebook Series*, London: Macmillan, pp. 185–205 (Originally published in Toni O'Brien Johnson and David Cairns (eds.) (1991), *Gender and Irish Writing*, Milton Keynes: Open University Press).

Crotty, Patrick (2001), "All I Believed That Happened There Was Revision", in Tony Curtis, *The Art of Seamus Heaney* (see separate entry), pp. 191–204.

Cruise O'Brien, Conor (1975), "A Slow North-East Wind", *The Listener*, 25 September, pp. 404–405.

Deane, Seamus (1985), "Seamus Heaney: the Timorous and the Bold", in Seamus Deane (1985), *Celtic Revivals*, London: Faber, pp. 174–186.

Deane, Seamus (1996), "Powers of Earth and Visions of Air", in Catharine Malloy and Phyllis Carey (1996), *Seamus Heaney: The Shaping Spirit*, Newark: University of Delaware Press, pp. 27–33.

Docherty, Thomas (1991), "Ana-; or Postmodernism, Landscape, Seamus Heaney", in Anthony Easthope and John O. Thompson (eds.) (1991), *Contemporary Poetry Meets Modern Theory*, Hemel Hempstead: Harvester Wheatsheaf, pp. 68–80.

Dunn, Douglas (2001), "Quotidian Miracles: *Seeing Things*" in Tony Curtis, *The Art of Seamus Heaney* (see separate entry), pp. 205–225.

Goodby, John and Ivan Phillips (2001), "Not Bad: *The Spirit Level*", in Tony Curtis, *The Art of Seamus Heaney* (see separate entry), pp. 241–260.

Kendall, Tim (2001), "An Enormous Yes?: *The Redress of Poetry*", in Tony Curtis, *The Art of Seamus Heaney* (see separate entry), pp. 227–239.

Lloyd, David (1981), "Seamus Heaney's *Field Work*", *Ariel*, XII (April), Volume 12, Number 2, pp. 87–92.

Lloyd, David (1993), "Pap for the Dispossessed: Seamus Heaney and the Poetics of Identity", in *Anomalous States* (1993), Dublin: Lilliput Press, pp. 13–40 (Reprinted in Elmer Andrews (ed.) (1992), *Seamus Heaney: A Collection of Critical Essays*, London: Macmillan, pp. 87–116).

Longley, Edna (1986), "*North*: 'Inner Emigré' or 'Artful Voyeur'?", *Poetry in the Wars*, Newcastle: Bloodaxe Books, pp. 140–169 (Also collected in Tony Curtis, *The Art of Seamus Heaney* (see separate entry), pp. 63–95).

Malloy, Catharine (1996), "Seamus Heaney's *Seeing Things*: 'Retracing the path back...'", in Catharine Malloy and Phyllis Carey (1996), *Seamus Heaney: The Shaping Spirit*, Newark: University of Delaware Press, pp. 157–173.

Malloy, Catharine and Phyllis Carey (1996), "Introduction" in Catharine Malloy and Phyllis Carey (1996), *Seamus Heaney: The Shaping Spirit*, Newark: University of Delaware Press, pp. 13–24.

Manganiello, Dominic (2000), "The Language of Exile: Heaney and Dante", *Canadian Journal of Irish Studies*, Vol. 26, Spring, pp. 101–113.

O'Brien, Eugene (1996), "Poetry, Prose and Politics in Northern Ireland", *Imprimatur*, Vol. 1, Nos. 2/3, pp. 142–150.

O'Brien, Eugene (1999a), "*North*: the Politics of Plurality", *Nua*, Vol. II, Nos. 1 & 2, Spring, pp. 1–19.

O'Brien, Eugene (1999b), "Seamus Heaney's Prose: Preoccupying Questions", in Bill Lazenbatt (ed.), *Writing Ulster: Northern Narratives*, No. 6, pp. 49–67.

Phillips, Helen (2001), "Seamus Heaney's *Beowulf* ", in Tony Curtis, *The Art of Seamus Heaney* (see separate entry), pp. 263–285.

Ricks, Christopher (1969), "Lasting Things", *The Listener*, 26 June, pp. 900–901.

Smith, Stan (1992), "Seamus Heaney: The Distance Between", in Corcoran, Neil (ed.), (1992), *The Chosen Ground: Essays on the Contemporary Poetry of Northern Ireland*, Bridgend, Mid Glamorgan: Poetry Wales Press, pp. 35–61.

Stevenson, Anne (2001), "The Peace Within Understanding: Looking at *Preoccupations*", in Tony Curtis, *The Art of Seamus Heaney* (see separate entry), pp. 129–137.

Vendler, Helen (2001), "Second Thoughts: *The Haw Lantern*", in Tony Curtis, *The Art of Seamus Heaney* (see separate entry), pp. 165–178.

Waterman, Andrew (1992), "The best way out is always through", in Elmer Andrews (ed.) (1992), *Seamus Heaney: A Collection of Critical Essays*, London: Macmillan, pp. 11–38.

Welch, Robert (1992), "'A rich young man leaving everything he had': Poetic Freedom in Seamus Heaney", in Elmer Andrews (ed.) (1992), *Seamus Heaney: A Collection of Critical Essays*, London: Macmillan, pp. 150–181.

Other Works Cited

Bakhtin, Mikhail (1981), *The Dialogic Imagination: Four Essays*, Translated by Caryl Emerson and Michael Holquist, Austin: University of Texas Press.

Benjamin, Walter (1977), *The Origin of German Tragic Drama*, Translated by John Osborne, London: New Left Books.

Derrida, Jacques (1989), *Of Spirit: Heidegger and the Question*, Translated by Geoffrey Bennington and Rachel Bowlby, Chicago: Chicago University Press.

Derrida, Jacques (1992), *Acts of Literature*, Edited by Derek Attridge, London: Routledge.

Eliot, T.S. (1963), *Collected Poems 1909–1962*, London: Faber.

Glob, P.V. (1969), *The Bog People: Iron Age Man Preserved*, London: Faber.

Jay, Martin (1984), *Adorno*, Fontana Modern Masters Series, General editor Frank Kermode, London: Fontana.

Joyce, James (1993), *A Portrait of the Artist as a Young Man*, Edited by R.B. Kershner, Boston: Bedford Books of St Martin's Press (First published 1916).

Kiberd, Declan (2000), *Irish Classics*, London: Granta.

Levinas, Emmanuel (1969), *Totality and Infinity: An Essay on Exteriority*, Translated by Alphonso Lingis, Pittsburgh: Duquesne University Press.

Levinas, Emmanuel (1981), "Ethics of the Infinite" in Richard Kearney (ed.), *Dialogues with Contemporary Continental Thinkers: The Phenomenological Heritage*, Manchester: Manchester University Press, pp. 49–69.

Levinas, Emmanuel (1989), *The Levinas Reader*, Edited by Seán Hand, Oxford: Basil Blackwell.

O'Brien, Eugene (2001), "Northern Ireland: The Omagh Bomb, Nationalism and Religion" in Meghan O'Meara (ed.) *History Behind the Headlines: The Origins of Conflicts Worldwide*, Volume 2, New York: Gale, pp. 221–235.

Shklovsky, Victor (1965), "Art as Technique", in Lee T. Lemon and Marion J. Reis, *Russian Formalist Criticism: Four Essays*, Lincoln: University of Nebraska Press.

Yeats, William Butler (1979), *The Collected Poems of William Butler Yeats*, London: Macmillan.

Index